WALKING
FOOTBALL

WALKING FOOTBALL
IMPROVE YOUR LIFE

TOM MORAN

Walking Football Association England Player

The Book Guild Ltd

First published in Great Britain in 2020 by
The Book Guild Ltd
9 Priory Business Park
Wistow Road, Kibworth
Leicestershire, LE8 0RX
Freephone: 0800 999 2982
www.bookguild.co.uk
Email: info@bookguild.co.uk
Twitter: @bookguild

Typeset in 11pt Minion Pro

Printed on FSC accredited paper
Printed and bound in Great Britain by 4edge Limited

ISBN 978 1913208 493

British Library Cataloguing in Publication Data.

A catalogue record for this book is available from the British Library.

For all the fantastic friends I have made through walking football. Thank you for all your help.

Special thanks to all who sent me articles and information about themselves, their teams and the game, both at home and abroad.

Thank you to Barnet walking football team.

Okay, so you have picked me up and want to know what it is all about. You may be over fifty and if, like me, you are over sixty and you have passed the milestone of vets, or even super vets football, and your body is telling you to slow down but your brain keeps urging you to kick a football again (if you've ever played football, you will know what I mean), I might be just what you need.

Walking football. One of the UK's fastest-growing sports, and growing fast worldwide.

So what do you get from walking football?

The old changing-room banter, meeting people who, if you relate a story from the '60s, '70s or '80s, know what you are talking about, the smell of Deep Heat. We are all really there for the same reason… To kick a ball around with some old and new friends, then a drink in the bar, then home sweet home. What could be better?

Being involved in our later years, trying to keep healthy and have fun is what walking football is all about.

If you love the game, want to know how to get fit and improve your physical and mental well-being, this is the book for you.

Learn how to get involved. An interesting, fun read.

Everything from your health and well-being to social prescribing to the beautiful game.

The game, the fun, your health, the facts – it's all here.

CONTENTS

FOREWORD

IF EVER THERE WAS A PASTIME THAT WAS MADE for an over-fifty football-loving person, walking football is pretty near perfect.

I would put it up there with the best inventions ever. For me, it has been fantastic.

What comes after retirement? Gardening, shopping with your partner, DIY. Holidays are good – but there must be more.

There is, and for me, walking football is it.

When I first read about the game, I was intrigued but did not really get it. After hearing about it on and off as the days went by, I thought it must be worth investigating.

I have always loved sport, particularly football, and really missed not playing, but walking football, come on, I'm not doing that!

Cutting to the quick, I was hooked after the first visit. I could see everything I read about the game was true: enjoyment, friendship, fitness, banter, physical and mental well-being.

I started to think about how the game linked in with a new NHS initiative: social prescribing.

I have always enjoyed reading books and have often thought how great it would be to write a book of my own.

Then, in a moment of madness, I thought, what if I wrote a book about walking football with other interesting facts included? So now I am giving it a go.

Hopefully this book will make you think more about your physical and mental well-being, and help you learn about social prescribing within the NHS. Oh yes, and give you an insight into the beautiful game of walking football, of course, with some interesting stories and a few laughs along the way.

So, I hope you enjoy it, and maybe it will persuade you to get your families, friends, neighbours or anybody, to think about their health as they get older. Give the game a try; I know you will love it.

Your health is your wealth.

Enjoy.

SID'S STORY

Sid Tobias, aged eighty-four. An inspiration to everyone. I met Sid when he arrived at Barnet for training. He sold me a dummy, and was away down the wing. A story he reminds me of nearly every week! Thanks, Sid.

Sid's journey is a great tale. I asked him for a few interesting bits about how he feels about walking football, and he sent me his life story. But it is so interesting I have had to put it in the book.

Thank you, Sid.

I WAS BORN AT CRUMPSALL HOSPITAL, Manchester, on October 12 1935, and lived the first two years of my life in Choir Street, near Strangeways prison. We were a poor family but managed to move to Crumpsall, where we were living when war broke out in 1939. We lived through the Blitz – the heavy and frequent bombing attacks on UK cities, ports and industrial areas – from September 1940 until May 1941. Due to my ill health and extreme allergic asthma, I was sent to the Jewish Fresh Air Home in Delemere Forest, Cheshire, an establishment for delicate Manchester and Salford children. They did not realise there were more allergy triggers there than in Manchester. Delemere was an idyllic spot and I played sport there with a passion.

We found out the war was over when we bumped into a group of Italian POWs in the forest.

Back in Manchester I managed to obtain a bursary to Manchester Grammar School, a stroke of good fortune.

I played in goal for the 'babes' first XI. As the next level was under-fourteens, who had four teams, I went down every Saturday morning to get a game for whoever was short of players. One Saturday I was asked to play in goal for our opponents, thus becoming the only Jewish boy to play for St Bede's Roman Catholic school, which ensured a welcome and a blessing from the priests whenever we played them. Turning up every week unselected meant I might play at any standard or in any position. I found out, to my amazement, I was a natural goalscorer, and was made the under-fourteen first XI centre-forward. I kept my first XI place right through school. We had a good side, beating Manchester Boys (hat-trick, all left foot), Oxford and Cambridge University joint touring team, and Royal Military Academy, Sandhurst, along the way, as well as a great record against other Manchester schools. I ended up top goalscorer. Ian Bailey was in charge of the first XI, along with a new gym master, Allen Wade, who was terrific.

Allen became head of coaching for England when Sir Alf Ramsey took over as England manager.

After Manchester Grammar School, I attended Manchester University, playing in the uni side on Wednesdays. I obtained a BSc in pharmacy.

Playing in the country-wide Pharmacy Department Cup, which my team, Manchester, won 4-1, was a big thrill, scoring a hat-trick in the final. Although our midfielder, Tom Fenoughty, was the brains of the team. Tom later played for Chesterfield, Sheffield United and was player/manager of Matlock Town. Tom and his two brothers are the only three siblings to play together in the same team in a Wembley final, when in 1975, Matlock Town defeated Scarborough 4-0.

I did my post-graduate year at Salford Royal Hospital, where Roger Byrne, the Manchester United and England captain who died in the Munich air disaster, was doing his physiotherapy course.

Saturday football

After leaving school I joined the old boys (Old Mancunians) who played in the Lancashire Amateur League. The league had three sections: North, South and Central, and up to four divisions in each section. Together with the I Zingari league, this was considered one of the highest standards of amateur football in the north-west. Most of the old boys' teams were full of lawyers, accountants and other professional people, who were earning up to three times as much as a top professional footballer (who earned about £12 for a win, £10 for a draw). It was full of good players who could not afford to take a pay cut to become a professional footballer!

In the days of not-so-good pitches and changing facilities, there were many good teams around, particularly YMCA, Middleton Amateurs and Whalley Range.

I had many enjoyable years playing for Old Mancs, mainly in the first and sometimes the seconds – we all have occasional loss of form, or the selection committee are incompetent!

I did not possess many skills in tight spaces and was hopeless in the air (nasty wet leather ball with thick laces giving me a headache), but I was very fast, always in space or heading for space. A cool, calm finisher, especially on one-on-ones with the keeper, and reading where the ball would finish in the six yard box.

In 1958, the Old Mancs were invited to Brionne in France for an Easter tour. We had a civic reception and a grand ball on Saturday and Sunday night. A cycle race, of course, and matches against FC Brionne and their big rivals Quevilly, from Rouen. I was nicknamed 'Un Locomotive'.

After beating Brionne 2-1 and Quevilly 4-1, which included a hat-trick for me, I was treated like a hero.

Quevilly reached the semi-finals of the French Cup a few years later.

The following year, Brionne were invited to Manchester and a civic reception held by the Lord Mayor was followed by a trip to Maine Road to see Manchester City versus WBA. A dinner at the Royal George in Knutsford followed. Very posh.

They were amazed when I told them I was not playing against them the next day. I was dropped. Astonishment! There was a quick meeting and they invited me to play for them, which I was honoured to do. Old Mancs winning 3-0. I became one of the first English players to play for a continental club, after John Charles in 1957, but before Denis Law in 1961.

I played many years for Old Mancs, never winning any trophies but making some good friends and having much enjoyment.

Sunday football

For ten years I was a soccer rebel. I started playing Sunday football about 1950, but the FA did not recognise Sunday football until 1960. I could have been suspended from playing on the other six days if discovered.

At aged fourteen/fifteen I was playing for Manchester Maccabi, the best Jewish team in Manchester. They played in the Salford Sunday League (open age with pub teams). I quickly learned to stay in space away from the centre-half, utilising my speed, and avoiding bad tackles and injury.

At a lower level were the main Jewish leagues. The Northern Jewish Soccer League (NJSL) had teams from Liverpool, Southport, Blackpool, Leeds, Sheffield and Manchester. After leaving Maccabi I joined The Shrubberies, where I helped the team win a cup, collecting my medal from one of my heroes, 'big Frank' Swift, the Manchester City and England goalkeeper. We also won the league championship.

I was lucky enough to be selected to represent the NJSL on a number of occasions and became the league's honorary secretary for a few years.

My biggest disappointment was not being selected to represent Great Britain in the Maccabiah Games in Israel. This is the Jewish version of the Olympics and covers many sports, with many countries competing. I was in the final trial in London on three occasions.

After my third effort, two of the selectors told me I played well and was a 'cert' to be selected. After a period of time, I was informed I did not make the squad. A big disappointment. Fifty years later I bumped into one of the selectors at the Manchester City versus Sunderland EFL Cup Final in 2014. His first words to me were, "Sid, I'm really sorry that you were cheated out of your Maccabiah place all those years ago." It hurts to this day. I kept playing, enjoying the game until I finally retired, aged forty-five.

Manchester City

I have been a City supporter as far back as I can remember. My first game was at Maine Road on Christmas Day, 1946, when they played Plymouth Argyle and won 4-3. Their next match was on the following day, Boxing Day, away at Plymouth (won 3-2)! I have had my ups and downs with City over the years, through the days of Bert Trautmann, Roy Paul, Don Revie, Colin Bell and many others.

On the non-playing side, I met lots of people: ex-Chairman Eric Alexander, who was my wingman for many years at Old Mancunians; Dr Norman Luft, one of my best friends, was the club doctor; and through our socialising, my wife and I met players such as Joe Corrigan and Dave Watson. For many years I lived five doors up from City and England full-back Jimmy Meadows, whose career was cut short when he was badly injured in the cup final against Newcastle. So I have a long connection with City, just to prove that I have not come out of the woodwork since Pep's arrival.

Walking Football

You are probably thinking that my wife Lyn must have great patience, putting up with all that football for all those years. You are right. It was Lyn who showed me an advert for walking football at Vale Farm, Wembley and said, "You should try that, it is right up your street."

So I did. There were only a few of us, and I was a good deal older than the others. We played four-a-side. I then went to Barnet, which is local to me nowadays, and numbers quickly grew. I have represented Barnet in competitons for the over-sixties and -sixty-fives and was recently invited to play in south-east England's over-seventies trials, giving about ten years to all other players.

My main assests of speed and 'fox in the box' are now denied to me in this form of the game, but finding space and being available, with accurate and well-weighted passes, are still very important. Think David Silva.

So, will you be fit enough to play?

I have a stent to keep one of my arteries open, due to high cholesterol, and take drugs for high blood pressure. I am bordering on diabetic, my back does not let me stand without a slight lean forward. I have had bilateral inguinal hernia repairs and four operations on my hands. My feet have about fifteen seed corns, which feels like walking on small, sharp stones, and these are dug out with a scalpel every few months.

I am fit to play walking football at eighty-four years, so I am pretty sure you are.

What do I get out of walking football? The thrill of competition, especially against younger men. The camaraderie, the friendships formed. The realisation you still retain some of your skills (downside, you've lost some). The thrill of hitting the back of the net.

The joy of playing football again.

I am quite moved by the reaction shown when I hit the turf (artificial), and the concern shown that the old man may have been injured.

So there you have it. You are saying to yourself, should I try this? The answer is YES.

CHAPTER ONE

THE NHS AND SOCIAL PRESCRIBING

THE NHS – WE LOVE YOU. I CAN HEAR YOU NOW: "I've just spent my hard-earned cash looking around for an interesting read, and my nice new book starts off with some stuff about the NHS. I love football and I want to read and learn about walking football, not the NHS."

Don't worry, folks, you will. Hopefully, after reading through the book, you will be enlightened about the opportunities available to every man and woman, whatever age, with regard to the beautiful game of walking football.

Please be patient. You may be able to make a difference. Here is a thought: if you can help just one person in life, how would that make you feel? For me, helping people is something I enjoy. I am surprised at this, as it has only recently happened. We will investigate more later.

I am now aged sixty-one. Up until the age of fifty, I barely knew the way to my doctor's surgery. Then I quickly learned the route, as I seemed to be going there on a fairly regular basis. This seems to be a regular talking point with my friends and family. Is it true that up to the age of fifty, your visits to the GP are relatively rare, but come fifty, you are almost on first-name terms with the doctor's receptionist?

Some of the ailments I have suffered over the last few years are: foot problems, knee problems, digestion problems, tennis elbow, a frozen shoulder, nasal problems, eye problems and high blood pressure.

I would imagine there are a fair few people reading this who are nodding their head, thinking, he has got it right. Equally, there are many of you laughing, thinking, I have got to over fifty with hardly any of the ailments mentioned. Good for you, but the point I am making is that if you have a medical problem, you know what to do and where to go. Please bear with me, read on, take some time to think about your NHS. Along with many people, I never really gave the NHS too much thought. They have always been there for me, my parents, my children and my friends.

Don't worry, the football stuff is coming. If your boots or trainers are hidden away, I am hoping to encourage you to get them on again.

When the NHS was formed by the Minister of Health at the time, Aneurin Bevan, in 1948, nobody realised how important it would become to us all.

It is there for everybody, rich or poor. The NHS has developed and expanded over the years and is an institution we all love.

Most people I know would do anything to help the NHS. I for one have always had great affection for it, and would do anything that could help, even in the smallest way.

The NHS is in crisis. This is a phrase that we all hear regularly from many media outlets.

The NHS is struggling to cope. Social care services are stretched to the limit. NHS finances are struggling. Cuts in local authority spending. How do we cope with an ageing population? GPs under pressure. Not enough nurses – these are just a few of the headlines we all see and hear about as we go about our daily lives.

We take the NHS for granted. At least I do.

One of the headlines that really got me thinking was 'An Ageing Population'.

When you are young, you are invincible; nothing seems to worry you. You feel you can do anything. When you are old, you become invisible.

The population is ageing, and the NHS will need to adapt.

The NHS cannot create a healthier society without our help.

This is something that should interest us all. How can we help people live healthier and more connected lives? Can we all do our bit to try to become healthier? Of course we can.

Social prescribing. What? I hear you say.

This is a new NHS initiative that can help.

Walking football – improve your life.

This is a sport that you can do to help yourself and, in turn, help the NHS.

Do something you enjoy. Improve your physical and mental well-being.

If you have never heard of social prescribing, read on. I know you will find this interesting. Can this help the NHS? Can this help you? Yes, is the answer.

Social Prescribing

Social Prescribing. What?! I can just hear you say, "What about the walking football stuff?" Don't worry, it is coming soon. Firstly, let me tell you about this wonderful idea. The NHS has published their long-term plan for healthcare in England. Over one thousand social prescribing link workers will be recruited by the end of 2020/21. They will work to help patients find suitable activities that are a better alternative to medication. The aims of social prescribing are to reduce the rise of healthcare costs and ease pressure on GPs. This is great news.

As Dr Vicky Simpson said when interviewed by ITV News, 'social prescribing will work for a wide range of people, including patients with one or more long-term conditions, who are lonely or isolated, or who have complex social needs which affect their well-being'.

NHS England is recruiting advisers to help patients live fitter, healthier lives, and combat loneliness, anxiety and depression.

Obviously there is a need for more evidence on the effectiveness of social prescribing, but hopefully it will lead to a reduction in GP appointments. Referrals to community services such as walking football, exercise, art classes and even ballroom dancing can boost health and well-being more than supplying pills or other treatments. Do you see where I am going with this?

The NHS England web site (www.england.nhs.uk) has reported that the social prescribing link workers will be able to talk to people and give them the time to talk about what matters to them in their life and support them to find an enjoyable outlet that could prove a better alternative than medication as part of a change in the provision of personal care.

Social prescribing pilot schemes are being trialled around the UK, with promising results. Some results show GPs now see twelve patients per session rather than fifteen, allowing the GP a bit more time with each patient; this is a positive result for social prescribing.

So what do you think? An interesting opening to your new book, I hope.

I have been playing walking football for three years now and I love it. As I played more and more, met many people, had lots of fun, I started to realise that the game is growing so much, and so quickly, who knows where it will be in, say, ten years' time.

I very quickly realised that there seemed to be a link between the game and the joy it gives to all participants. This realisation prompted me to delve deeper into mental and physical health and well-being, the NHS, and social prescribing. The connection was staring me in the face. This led me to start thinking, how could I get this message over to fellow walking footballers all over the country? It is great sending messages, texts and emails; Facebook is great if you are interested in the social media side of things, but not everybody has the time or inclination to surf the net. But a nice book, that is different.

I have not counted how many teams, let alone how many players, are playing this version of the beautiful game, but the number is big! One estimate states there are over 1,200 teams and 40,000 players. The game is growing fast. I suspect the number is bigger.

Before the main course, can I leave you with a few thoughts: if you enjoy football and would like to get a little bit fitter, if you would like to improve your physical and mental well-being, if you want to meet people and have some fun – walking football is definitely for you, I promise.

If you already play the game, could you introduce someone else to the fold? Perhaps you know a relative, friend or neighbour who could benefit from the game?

You could make a big difference to someone else's life and in turn help the NHS too. I have done this, and it makes me feel good about myself.

Remember the saying: your health is your wealth.

Have you ever thought about walking Football?

SOCIAL PRESCRIBING EXAMPLE:
An article by healthierfleetwood.co.uk

David Gore, who is communications officer for Healthier Fleetwood and is also a player with the local Fleetwood Flyers walking football team, has highlighted to me a fantastic example of how social prescribing works in a local community. Hopefully many other areas can learn from what Fleetwood are doing. I for one would love to see this initiative investigated more by the powers that be. I hope this book can help highlight some new thinking along the way.

Fleetwood, a coastal town in Lancashire, have delivered a resident-focused independent initiative which brings together all the local organisations, groups, activities and events that encourage people to take more control of their health and well-being.

Healthier Fleetwood are the designated pathway for social prescribing in Fleetwood and have always worked very closely with Fleetwood Flyers, the local walking football team. As we all know, walking football is an excellent activity for improving physical and mental well-being.

Healthier Lancashire & South Cumbria Integrated Care System, (www.healthierlsc.co.uk), are a partnership which joins up health and care services, have said statistics showed residents in Fleetwood could expect to live shorter lives and experience more life-changing illnesses than people elsewhere in the country and, in fact, even those a few miles away on the Fylde coast.

Residents, voluntary, faith and community groups, health professionals, the emergency services, local authority representatives, and business leaders met and found there was a shared desire that something should be and could be done.

The early months of Healthier Fleetwood were spent connecting the many parties in the town already doing fantastic work in the community, often unknown to the majority of residents. One of their main aims was to connect the community. So while their partnerships developed, the question remained: how do they make a difference? The discussion has moved to include education, employment, training, the environment; these are important areas, but for now the focus is at grassroots level – helping individuals make a positive difference to their lives and their families, and that is happening.

The country has a growing movement of 'health creation', residents taking more control over their lives, becoming the do-ers, rather than the done-to.

Well done, Fleetwood. What a great story, and good luck to Fleetwood Flyers Walking Football team.

If you would like to have a try at walking football in the Fleetwood area, contact Heywood Sports Village. Details can be found in Chapter Five.

Thank you so much for reading up to this point. I am now ready to give you what you want with regard to the greatest game: walking football. The facts, the fun, the teams; it's all coming your way.

KEITH'S STORY

MY NAME IS KEITH TYRRELL. I AM SIXTY-SEVEN years young and I play walking football for Midsomer Norton on Tuesdays and Thursdays, at a cost of £4 per game.

The group was set up in 2015 and I joined in August 2018 following open heart surgery in February of the same year.

I had the misfortune of having three heart attacks over a four-day period in January 2018, which resulted in requiring a double heart bypass fairly urgently.

The operation was not only life-saving but also life-changing, which is my legacy of today. Following the operation I spent the next six months slowly recovering, unable to return to normality due to not only a lack of strength and energy, but also being devoid of confidence, which was leading towards depression.

My life up to the operation was quite hectic, as I was the mayor of Radstock, which was a demanding role within the community. I also worked on a casual basis for a few of the local funeral directors. This made me a reasonably well-known figure in the local area, as it was a high-profile existence.

By the June of 2018 I realised that I could not return to my former life, so I resigned from both of my positions, which left a gaping hole to be filled; with what, I didn't have a clue.

Going into rehab in mid-June started me on the road to recovery, where I started to build not only my physical strength, but also my mental strength and the ability to reconnect with people following a reclusive six-month period.

I was introduced to walking football by my wife, who was made aware of the sport by someone in her social group.

Being an avid football fan and player from a bygone age, playing at a reasonable level, I decided to give it a go; although I had reservations if I would be able to blend in with the players and if my stamina would hold out.

For the first couple of weeks, I suffered from beginner's muscle aches and pains, together with extreme tiredness. But, never being one to quit, I continued to put maximum effort in every session, which culminated in a massive improvement to my fitness levels and a return of confidence, due to my achievement following my journey through surgery.

The camaraderie the group has is fantastic, and although we are competitive on the pitch, after the game we enjoy a coffee and a natter, putting the world to right, and comparing war wounds all over the body. We actually care for one another, and we help each other out in times of need; this is reinforced by our social gatherings outside of football, which are very well attended by many of us.

I can honestly say that walking football has changed my life and is now the focal point of my recreation outside of my home life. It has given me a purpose to get up in the morning and go out and enjoy life again and enjoy the company of like-minded old fellows like myself.

I can thoroughly recommend walking football to anyone who wants to enjoy playing in the fresh air, join in with the relentless good-humoured banter, getting fitter and feeling better about yourself all round, regardless of if you've played before.

CHAPTER TWO

WALKING FOOTBALL – WHAT'S IT ALL ABOUT?

WALKING FOOTBALL IS BECOMING QUITE A phenomenon. Let me try to explain about how the game has come to be one of the fastest-growing sports in the UK. I am hoping as we go along this journey, for those not already playing, your interest will increase and you will feel the need to have a go. I can assure you, once you try it, you will be hooked.

Although we think of walking football as a modern game, the first match ever played was back in 1932 between Derby Railway and Crewe Railway. The game took place at Derby County's Baseball Ground, a stadium which some of you may remember.

Derby County now play at Pride Park, but I remember fondly the days at the Baseball Ground: Roy McFarland, Colin Todd and Archie Gemmill. What a team. Oh yes, and Mr Clough.

The game pretty much disappeared from view until 2011 when Chesterfield FC Community Trust, led by John Croot, decided to form a team called Chesterfield Senior Spireites. John is widely regarded as the man who invented the game. More about John later.

The plan was to help over-fifties in the local area to try their hand at the game, and it worked!

Walking football is great for people who have played the game since childhood, but now, due to age or aching bones, feel they need a slower version of the game.

But it is also aimed at people not involved in football but who would like some social interaction. There is a place for everybody, male or female. If you want some competitive elements, you can have them. If you are not so interested in this side of the game, then you will also be welcomed with open arms to enjoy the fun and camaraderie. The sport can be played both indoors and out. Typically, games are six- or seven-a-side.

Although it is based on association football, the big difference is that if a player runs, they concede a free kick to the other side. This restriction, together with a ban on slide tackles, is aimed at avoiding injuries and helping those who are physically disadvantaged. The manner in which the sport is played promotes cardiovascular fitness whilst producing less stress on the body. It also helps players maintain an active lifestyle. There are lots more rules involved, which we will look at along the way. The sport came to wider public attention after a Barclays advert in 2014.

WFA Laws of the Game
Courtesy of thewfa.co.uk

Introduction

This revised edition of the WFA 'Laws of the Game' acknowledges that this unique sport is evolving and developing as it grows, but nevertheless holds fast to the basic ethos and values of the game: "To ensure all matches are played safely with full consideration of every participant's age, gender and ability."

It is therefore expected that all players, managers and club members will conduct themselves accordingly, respecting all fellow participants, including referees and other match officials. Failure to do so is likely to result in disciplinary action, including disqualification of individuals and/or clubs from WFA events.

Section A:
   Players, Pitches and Equipment

Although it is likely that tournaments, leagues, competitions and events will have bespoke rules and conditions, all matches played under the auspices of the WFA will comply with the following standards.

Players

1. Goalkeepers must be clearly distinguishable from outfield players on either team.
2. Substitutes must be clearly distinguishable from players on either team, until they are called into play.
3. A match should be abandoned if a team is permanently reduced to below the minimum number of players. The term 'permanently' does not apply, however, to players who have been sin-binned but does apply to players who are unable to play through injury or receiving a red card. The minimum number of players per format is:
   - Five-a-side matches – minimum of three players.
   - Six-a-side matches – minimum of four players.
   - Seven-a-side matches – minimum of four players.
4. A team which causes the abandonment of a match will forfeit it.

Pitches

5. The standard pitch dimensions for competition (i.e. five-a-side, six-a-side and seven-a-side) are a width between twenty-five metres (min) and thirty-seven metres (max), and a length between thirty-five metres (min) and fifty-five

metres (max). It is acknowledged, however, that pitches at some facilities may fall outside these guidelines, in which case it is a matter for the referee to decide whether or not to proceed.

6. The standard goal size for such competitions is a width between three metres (min) and five metres (max) and a height between 1.2 metres and two metres (max). It is acknowledged, however, that goals at some facilities may fall outside these guidelines, in which case it is a matter for the referee to decide whether or not to proceed.

7. A goal area must be clearly marked at each end of the pitch. This may be a semi-circle or rectangle and should extend between four metres (min) and six metres (max) from the goal line.

8. A clearly marked penalty spot should be positioned in line with the centre of the goal and six metres from the goal line.

9. The position of the ball on the pitch is determined when it crosses a line entirely (i.e. the whole of the ball). A ball located on the line marking the goal area is considered to be within that area and can, therefore, only be played by the goalkeeper.

Section B: Foul Play
Running and Jogging

1. Running or jogging on or off the ball is not permitted by any player (including goalkeepers) and will usually result in an indirect free kick

being awarded. If, in the opinion of the referee, such conduct results in a clear goalscoring opportunity being denied, then the offending players should be removed from play for two minutes (blue card) and a penalty kick considered if the offending player is a goalkeeper.

2. The referee shall have sole interpretation on deciding what is and what is not walking. A walking action will generally be determined as a progression of steps throughout which there is constantly at least one foot in contact with the ground; both feet are momentarily grounded with the advancing leg straightened.

Ball Above Head Height

3. The ball is not permitted to travel above head height:
    - The ball should be deemed dead once it has exceeded head height.
    - Head height is defined as 1.83 metres or the height of the goal cross bar, which should not exceed two metres. (See *Section A: subsection 6.*)
    - The whole of the ball must exceed head height to be deemed an infringement.
    - The referee shall have sole interpretation on the ball exceeding head height.
    - A player commits a foul if they cause the ball to travel above head height.

- A player commits a foul if the ball deflects off them and goes above head height.
- A player commits a foul if they play the ball off a barrier and it exceeds head height.
- If a ball deflects off the goal frame and exceeds head height, it is not regarded as a foul, but the ball must immediately be deemed dead and retained by the goalkeeper.
- If a ball deflects off the goalkeeper in the process of making a save and exceeds head height before returning to play, it is not regarded as a foul, but the ball must immediately be deemed dead and retained by the goalkeeper.
- If a ball deflects off the goalkeeper in the process of making a save and exceeds head height, but then drops into the goal, a goal should be awarded.
- If a ball deflects off the goalkeeper in the process of making a save and exceeds head height, but then directly leaves the field of play, a corner or kick-in should be awarded, depending at which point the ball crossed the line.

Physical Contact

4. Physical contact is not permitted and is therefore regarded as foul play.

    The term 'physical contact' includes:

- Tackling across a player at a barrier.

- Blocking or cornering a player against a barrier.
- Crowding (two players versus one) a player against a barrier.
- Shoulder charging, pushing or barging.
- Stepping across or obstructing an opponent to gain an advantage or deny that player access to the ball or to a position.

Dangerous or Reckless Conduct

5. Deliberate dangerous or reckless conduct, regardless of whether or not there is any physical contact, should be regarded as 'aggravated' foul play.

Goal Area Infringements

6. An outfield player entering the goal area (unless they do so purely as a result of momentum) commits a foul, regardless of whether or not they play the ball.

7. A goalkeeper leaving the goal area during play commits a foul, *except* when this is a result of momentum only and providing that he/she is not in possession of the ball (and does not play the ball) outside the goal area.

8. The line marking the goal area is considered to be within that area for the purpose of identifying goal area infringements.

Other Infringements

9. A player commits a foul if they deliberately head the ball.
10. A player commits a foul by slide tackling and/or slide blocking.
11. A player commits a foul by tackling an opposing player (or poaching) from behind, regardless of whether there is any physical contact.
12. Any player – other than a goalkeeper – commits a foul if they deliberately play the ball with their hand or arm.
13. A player commits a foul if they fail to take a free kick, penalty, kick-in, kick-off or corner in accordance with the rules or as instructed by the referee.
14. A player commits a foul if they take a free kick, penalty, kick-in, kick-off or corner whilst the ball is moving.
15. A player commits a foul if they take a kick-in whilst the ball is not behind the line which marks the pitch area.
16. A player commits a foul if they hold onto a barrier in order to shield the ball or obstruct an opposing player, unless such contact is necessary to prevent a collision or to maintain balance.
17. Any player – other than a goalkeeper – commits a foul if they deliberately play the ball whilst they are on the ground (i.e. having any part of their body other than their feet on the pitch).

18. A goalkeeper commits a foul if they deliberately play the ball other than by throwing it under-arm or kicking it from the ground.

Section C: Sanctions
Free Kicks

1. All incidents of foul play are worthy of a free kick being awarded against the offending player's team.
2. All free kicks are indirect and should be taken at the location of the infringement, with opposing players being at least three metres from the ball.
3. A player taking a free kick is not permitted to take more than one step immediately prior to striking the ball. The ball should not be kicked with undue force or in a manner likely to cause injury.
4. A goal will only be allowed following a free kick once the ball has been played by another player. This does not include a direct shot at goal which deflects into the goal off another player or the goalkeeper.
5. There are, however, a number of exceptions for free kicks:
    • If a goalkeeper is deemed to have deliberately caused the ball to exceed head height, an indirect free kick should be awarded to the opposing team three metres outside the goal

area, adjacent to where the infringement occurred.

- If a goalkeeper is deemed to have deliberately played the ball other than by throwing it under-arm or kicking it from the ground, an indirect free kick should be awarded to the opposing team three metres outside the goal area, adjacent to where the infringement occurred.
- If a goalkeeper leaves the goal area during play, a penalty kick should be awarded to the opposing team. This does not apply when the goalkeeper leaves the area as a result of momentum only, providing he/she is not in possession of (and does not play) the ball outside the goal area.
- If an outfield player enters the goal area they are defending (unless they do so purely as a result of momentum), regardless of whether or not they play the ball. A penalty kick should be awarded to the opposing team.
- Free kicks awarded to an attacking team must not be taken within three metres of their opponents' goal area, but must be moved back accordingly, directly in line to where the infringement occurred.

Penalty Kicks

6. A penalty kick is a direct free kick.
7. A player taking a penalty kick is permitted to take only one step immediately prior to striking the ball.
8. A player in the process of taking a penalty kick commits a foul if they initially simulate striking the ball, in order to cause the goalkeeper to move in a specific direction.
9. When facing a penalty kick, a goalkeeper is permitted to move any part of their body and to travel along the goal line, but is not permitted to advance off the goal line prior to the kick being taken; this should result in the retaking of a saved or missed penalty.
10. All players, other than the goalkeeper defending the penalty kick, must be behind the ball immediately prior to the kick being taken.

Blue Card and Red Card Infringements

11. If a player commits three infringements (totting up) for running, foul play or a combination of both, the referee should show a blue card and cause them to leave the game (sin-bin) for two minutes.
    - A player receiving such a sanction must miss two minutes of playing time.
    - If a player returning from the sin-bin commits a further three infringements, the

referee should cause them to play no further part in the game (sent off).

- The referee shall have sole discretion to determine which infringements are worthy of 'totting up'. For example, causing the ball to travel above head height may not necessarily warrant such action.

12. If a player is guilty of deliberate dangerous or reckless conduct, this amounts to 'aggravated' foul play and the referee should, in such circumstances, show a red card and cause them to play no further part in the game (sent off) and, if applicable, the competition.

13. If a player (including an off-field substitute) uses threatening, abusive or insulting words or behaviour towards any other player, a referee, an official or any other participant, the referee should show a red card and cause them to play no further part in the game (sent off) and, if applicable, the competition.

Section D: Starting, Stopping and Continuing Play
Starting a Match

1. A coin toss shall be used at the start of a game to determine whether a team wishes to kick-off or choose which end they wish to attack. The team winning the toss is granted first choice.

2. The match shall commence only when the referee blows the whistle.

3. A goal cannot be scored directly from a kick-off, even in the event of a deflection into the goal from an opposing player or the goalkeeper. The goal should be disallowed and a free kick awarded to the opposing team.

Stopping and Resuming Play

4. If the referee stops play by blowing the whistle, play should only be resumed upon a further blow of the whistle. Quick free kicks (for example), without a referee's whistle to resume play, are not permitted. Referees are not obliged to delay play any longer than they feel necessary and, if safe do to so, may blow the whistle to restart a game immediately after a free kick has been awarded.

5. A drop ball may be used to resume play when it is not possible to determine which team should have possession – for example, following a sudden halt in play caused through injury.

6. A kick-in shall resume play (on pitches with touchlines) at the point where the ball left the field of play.

7. A corner kick shall resume play (on pitches with goal lines) on the same side of the pitch that the ball left the field of play.

Continuing Play

8. Goalkeepers may distribute the ball when grounded.
9. Unlimited back passes between a player and goalkeeper are permitted.
10. Goalkeepers can handle the ball directly from a back pass.
11. Goals may be scored by any player (except a goalkeeper) from any outfield position. In the event of a goalkeeper scoring, the goal should be disallowed, and the ball (deemed dead) retained by the opposing goalkeeper.

Kick-ins and Corners

12. Kick-ins and corners are indirect, with opposing players being at least three metres from the ball. A goal will only be allowed following a kick-in or corner once the ball has been played by another player: direct shots at goal from a kick-in or corner are not permitted and any such goals will be disallowed, even if deflected in off another player (goalkeeper included).
13. A player executing a kick-in or corner is not permitted to take more than one step immediately prior to striking the ball. The ball should not be kicked with undue force or in a manner likely to cause injury.

Playing an advantage

14. Although the decision to play an advantage can depend on many circumstances, WFA referees are advised to only take such action if:
    - It benefits the team which did not commit the infringement.
    - It is safe to do so and unlikely to result in a confrontation, especially following physical contact.

    Referees should clearly indicate that an advantage is being allowed and also ensure that they take the appropriate remedial action (blue card, warning/ advice) when it is safe and appropriate to do so.

Section E: Safety

1. Players must refrain from openly wearing jewellery or watches. Tape may be used to cover rings.
2. All players must wear shin pads, covered by their socks.

Walking Football

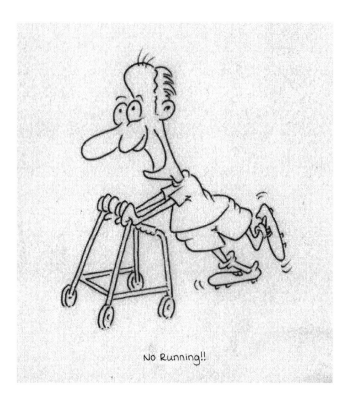

No Running!!

KEVIN'S STORY

I FIRST HEARD ABOUT WALKING FOOTBALL WHEN A friend from Portugal visited, saying how it was 'all the rage over there'. The idea seemed good, I thought, but would never catch on in the UK.

Six months later, I noticed that Barnet FC was running – sorry, I mean walking – Friday afternoon sessions for over-fifties. Unfortunately for me at the time I was working Monday to Friday nine to five, so I could not pursue this. Later in the year, I was delighted to hear Thursday evening sessions were starting. This concept I thought would be good for fitness levels, so my wife Olivia decided to join me. The first session was three-a-side and with a rush goalie. My biggest problem was running, and I was struggling. Then in successive sessions we both had finger injuries that needed treatment at Edgware Hospital walk-in centre (the nickname for our game changed to walk-in centre football). Shortly after this, my wife retired, and I was beginning to think this was not for me.

I persisted, remained injury-free, learned how to play, while walking most of the time. The Thursday-night sessions began to thrive and I found myself really enjoying the game. Then I became available to join the Friday sessions, so football on two days became part of my weekly routine.

The idea of playing in tournaments was mentioned. Our first game was against an experienced Orient team. We had a combined age of 160 for our two strikers. I was in defence and we were bravely holding on for a draw, and with the last kick of game there was a whistle. I stopped, they scored – the whistle was from other pitch. I was devastated.

Better times ahead as the Barnet squad gained more depth and my skills improved. We have played and beaten Arsenal at the Emirates, Tottenham at White Hart Lane, but my favourite moment was at the Olympic Stadium. At short notice we were asked to form an extra team in a three-way tournament between West Ham and Crystal Palace before their league game. I captained a scratch side on the morning after our Christmas party. We ended up winning both games 1-0.

The main thrill I have is just putting on the shirt and representing our team, something I could only dream of. I am still enjoying the training sessions and the camaraderie.

It has been a privilege to have facilitated many charity events through our games evenings. Age UK, Dementia Club UK and MIND, all charities close to our hearts, have all benefitted from these events.

Chapter Three

The Walking Football Association

THE WALKING FOOTBALL ASSOCIATION WAS
launched in December 2016. Their purpose is to
promote and facilitate the playing of walking football
as a unique amateur sport in the UK for the purpose of
recreation, physical exercise and competition.

Aiming to raise the profile of the game and seeking
to have an impact on physical and mental well-being are
part of their mission, and to maintain a high standard of
competitive play, leading to success on the national stage.

The game's growth was highlighted in May 2018,
when England staged the first-ever international games,
taking on Italy at the Amex Stadium, Brighton. The WFA

England over-fifties team won 2-0 and the over-sixties won 3-0. Tommy Charlton, younger brother of 1966 World Cup winners Bobby and Jack, was given his international debut at age seventy-two. The success of the event led to more international games versus Wales and Gibraltar.

In June 2019, a European Nations Cup took place at Chesterfield's Proact Stadium, featuring England, Wales and Italy, at both over-fifties and over-sixties. Wales and Italy have formed very good sides and were looking for a good showing against England.

Both England teams have very strong squads. Twenty players in each group made up from teams up and down the country.

England ran out worthy winners of both age groups. A fantastic achievement by both teams, and managers Paul Murtagh and Stuart Langworthy.

England over-fifties squad.

Paul Carr, founder and chief executive of the Walking Football Association, is very proud of the WFA's achievements so far and has big plans for the future.

Paul commented, "I played walking football for three years for Wigan Walkers and thoroughly enjoyed it. One thing I noticed quickly was that everywhere we played there seemed to be different rules, which was pretty frustrating for all involved. I started thinking about how I could improve things, so I set up the Walking Football Association.

England over-sixties squad.

"We have a set of rules which include no running, no contact, all free kicks are indirect and the ball cannot go over head height.

"The no-contact and no-running make it an inclusive game, with players from fifty to ninety years of age able to compete with each other.

"A great sport which helps older people get involved and continue to enjoy life".

On their web-site the WFA say that walking football offers a multitude of health benefits to older people such as reducing the risk of cardiovascular disease and stroke while improving blood pressure. Positive changes in postural balance, and resting heart rate, plus lowered cholesterol, improved blood sugar levels, and improving reactions, whilst slashing the odds of suffering from type 2 diabetes – all indicators of general good health.

Walking football is an excellent way of staying fit and healthy. Studies have shown it can be effective in the treatment of mild to moderate hypertension and that it can produce high aerobic activity with marked improvements in fat oxidation and aerobic power. Importantly, benefits are felt whilst deriving enjoyment, which makes people far more likely to exercise than perhaps the perceived chore of having to just 'exercise regularly'.

There are also many psychological and mental health advantages to playing walking football – namely high levels of personal reward and satisfaction with reduced levels of stress and exertion while playing, despite working physically hard.

Walking football also gives an often isolated section of the community the chance to become involved in something they really enjoy, make new friends, form lasting relationships with like-minded people and generally improve their social circle and overall quality of life, often making them feel less isolated and more a part of the wider community.

There are also significant benefits for any older people involved in a walking football environment or club who perhaps don't always want to play but can engage in other aspects of the sport or club such as administrative roles, team manager, organising fixtures, or sitting on a management committee of the club or even just being involved in a social capacity for the good company and friendship. All these things can help to keep older people mentally active and give their lives a very real sense of purpose and belonging, the value of which cannot be overstated.

As we get older, many of us struggle with our balance, strength, stamina, weight and worst of all, confidence and self-esteem levels, but walking football has the potential to make a significant impact in all these areas, building body strength, improving muscles, core stability and hopefully losing some of the weight usually gained during the ageing process. As well as being able to increase fitness levels, emotional health gets a great boost too for a person involved in walking football, not least self-confidence and self-esteem.

WFA — MOVING FORWARD

With both the over-fifties and over sixties men's teams looking good, the WFA are now moving on to the over-seventies. Dr Gareth Lewis has recently been named as manager. Gareth has been involved in football all of his life. Having played representative schools' football, he went on to play youth and amateur football for Nottingham Forest and Aston Villa.

Gareth has a UEFA 'B' coaching licence and has coached Nottingham City Boys teams for many years.

Good luck to Gareth in his new role.

The WFA have also got big plans for the women's game. Successful trials have been held for the over-forties and over-fifties, and two squads have now been formed. More on the women's game later.

WFA REFEREES

The WFA have been running an intensive referees' course since September 2017. The course has been developed by players and referees, endorsed by ex-premier league referee Uriah Rennie, and is delivered by professional trainers.

Source: thewfa.co.uk

WFA ENGLAND MANAGER
– OVER-FIFTIES

Paul Murtagh

Christine Murtagh

WITH MY FOOTBALL PARTICIPATION CUT SHORT at the age of fifteen through a serious knee injury, I rediscovered my passion for the game through walking football. In 2014 I joined forces with a friend, Matt Corp, to rejuvenate and restore an ailing tennis club in Birmingham. With the threat of closure, we decided to diversify into sports other than tennis. After watching the Barclays advert on TV, we set about starting walking football and used it as the catalyst for further potential expansion into walking sports at the club. Walking netball and cricket were trialled, but it was football, unsurprisingly, that turned out to be the most popular. Our open-door, all-inclusive policy saw us grow over the next five years. Now operating over twenty mixed sessions, from two sites per week, for all age groups and abilities, including our less mobile programme and our ladies-only sessions. We have set out to create a welcoming platform for anyone to give it a go, and subsequently reap the rewards and benefits from Britain's fastest-growing sport.

Our policy was to focus primarily on just getting people playing again, but due to the desire of many of the players, I branched out into playing friendlies against anyone I could find that were also facilitating the game. Obviously the competitive element is never too far away from any sport and walking football is no exception. In 2014, there were no other clubs in Birmingham, so we had to travel to the Black Country for our first competitive fixture against Hartshill Strollers, who had started about the same time as us. From there we travelled further afield to play against other clubs, including tournaments, but also to forge links and make new walking football friends.

Word of mouth and pulling from a large suburban area helped us grow and subsequently we became more successful on the competitive scene. In 2017, the club won almost every major tournament, only the People's Cup eluding us, finishing as beaten finalists.

When the newly formed Walking Football Association advertised for the England manager's role in 2017, it seemed a natural progression, so I applied for the role. As a life-long England fan that is passionate about walking football, the job was just too tempting to ignore. A true honour and a testament to where the game has come in such a short space of time, as England once again lead the way in developing a new sport for the world to enjoy.

While I am immensely proud to have led the England team out in the first-ever competitive international fixture against another nation, I am even more proud that I have had the opportunity to be involved in developing this game from such an early stage. I firmly believe that few people retire from playing football because they no longer enjoy it; in most cases they stop because they feel that the standard game is not appropriate for them anymore or injuries have taken their toll. Walking football prolongs the active involvement in a sport that most thought had passed them by. I love the ethos behind the game and I get a buzz from seeing the enjoyment and fulfilment it brings to so many.

I think the sport still has enormous potential. The more people that discover the game, the more it will grow. I feel that the vast majority of people that try it, love it, and that applies to people of all ages. Doing a form of exercise that people actually enjoy will only increase the numbers.

As a result, I think we will see a bigger, more established league structure that spans over larger areas. I think we will see competitive leagues in more varied age groups, including the emergence of younger players in the over-thirty-five and -forty age groups and an increase in the women's game. The game may morph into slightly different playing formats for the varied ages and even play with different rules, but it would all have stemmed from walking football. The popularity will increase not just in this country but in other countries (in some form), and an increase on a more competitive international stage would be exciting. Professional clubs will take more of a prominent role in the community and competitive side, health organisations and the NHS will link with local walking football groups as standard procedure. The powers that be need to be united, so we are all well placed to drive this massive growth forward. Who knows, Olympic sport!?

Walking football for all.

WFA ENGLAND MANAGER
– OVER-SIXTIES

STUART LANGWORTHY

England manager, Stuart Langworthy, right,
pictured with his son and England coach, Ross.

Judith Langworthy

57

ENGLAND OVER-SIXTIES MANAGER STUART Langworthy, who plays for Abbeymead Rovers in Gloucestershire, where he is chairman, secretary, walking football and super vets manager, was thrilled to be offered the England job back in 2017, and has done a fantastic job, guiding the team to win the WFA European Nations Cup.

Stuart, fifty-seven, saw an advert for the position of England manager and thought it seemed a good idea to apply.

After forty-four years volunteering in the game, it seemed an exciting opportunity and he thought it was a good fit for him.

One of Stuart's first tasks was to organise trials around the country with the aim of getting a twenty-man squad together to form an England team. Club managers around the country were asked to nominate players who they thought were good enough to trial and get a chance to play for their country.

His management team organised trials in London, Birmingham, Burnley and Cirencester. One of his main aims was to look for skilled players who also play the game the correct way. Stuart says, "There is no point selecting players who run all the time, or who are overly physical. Getting a sin-bin will not help the team. It is a very intelligent game, and a player with a good touch and intelligent movement can create the space needed. What I look for is technical ability for the position they play, positive team spirit and attitude, and somebody who is proud to represent their country."

Some tough decisions were taken along the way to create an England squad of twenty players. After settling on his squad, Stuart arranged training days with the aim of being ready for the first walking football international against Italy at the Amex Stadium, Brighton, which was played in June 2018.

A very proud day for all involved saw England over-fifties winning 2-0 and the over-sixties winning 3-0. The teams have never looked back since that day, securing victories over Wales and Gibraltar along the way. The highlight so far has been winning the European Nations Cup against Wales and Italy in June 2019. The next challenge for Stuart and the team will be the 2020 World Cup, being held in Manchester in May, which will have teams from all around the globe competing.

So for Stuart and his team, it is onwards and upwards. England took an over-fifty and over-sixty international team to Crete in October 2019 for international games against Greece. Stuart made his international debut playing for the over-fifties.

Amazing.

Chapter Four

How I Got Involved in the Game

I RECENTLY REACHED THE GRAND OLD AGE OF sixty. "How did I get here?" As Michael Caine once said after reaching the age of eighty-three, "Yesterday I was thirty-five, what has happened?" I am pretty sure this is a sentiment that is common to many older people. What can you do? Time and tide waits for no man. The process of nature continues, no matter how much we would like it to stop.

Life after sixty can be a challenging and uncertain time for some. It can also be fantastic and rewarding. Travel, relax, golf, shopping! Playing walking football. I know what I am doing.

I was lucky enough to have retired a few years ago. Having worked in the rat race of London for national newspapers for many years, I had to admit the stress and strain of the job got to me. Travelling by tube every day, having a responsible position; I am pretty sure I was a victim of burn-out. Having problems with my mum and her health, bringing up two great kids, feeling stressed, I had had enough. I was lucky to be able to talk to a fantastic boss and explain how I was feeling. The saying 'a problem shared is a problem halved' could never have been truer for me. The newspaper industry was always looking to cut costs. So I was lucky enough to negotiate an early retirement.

On a visit to the doctor, I explained how I was feeling. He was fairly sympathetic but basically told me do more exercise, get more hobbies, go and enjoy yourself. I would have been the perfect candidate to see a social prescriber, had they been invented. I did feel I was wasting the doctor's time.

Luckily I got back to normal fairly quickly, without the need for treatment, which was good news.

I am sure this episode of my life may strike a chord with a few of you. The moral of the story really is, if you are not feeling how you used to feel psychologically, talk to somebody – family, friends, doctors, they are all there for you. Do not feel you have to face life alone; there is always somebody who will help you. The social prescribing initiative is fantastic. Find out some more information about it. You never know, you may need it at some point in your life.

For generations, there was an assumption that life after sixty was when you really started your physical decline. Probably true, but you can still continue to feel good by staying physically active. You don't have to join a fancy gym; there are plenty of ways to attempt to stay in shape as you get older. A good saying I have always adhered to is 'why put off till tomorrow what you can do today?' Walking is a great start for everybody. Plan a basic goal of having a walk and try to increase the distance every week. How simple is that? Talk to your doctor before starting a new exercise plan. Depending upon your health and lifestyle, there might be some exercises that are better than others.

Did you know that things happen to your brain when you reach sixty? You start to slow down, but it is gradual.

You suddenly realise that you cannot do the things you used to. But you have to keep mind and body active.

This is why it is imperative you get a hobby. Healthy people have hobbies. Walking football is one such hobby.

I have always loved football; my mum stopped me sleep-walking when I was six, dressed in my football kit, going out the front door. If I heard her tell that story once, I heard it a million times. On family occasions, I used to plead with her not to tell the story, again.

I played with a lot of excellent young players in my early years. My first team was Colindale Eagles (pictured on the previous page), all boys from around the north-west London area.

Moving on to teenage years, Princes Park, another team with good young players; most had trials with big London, clubs, but all came up short in the end. When I was fourteen I had a couple of trials at Watford FC. I got the bus from Hendon to Watford on Sunday mornings; how nerve-wracking, turning up at Vicarage Road on my own with my Gola bag and Adidas Santiago boots. From there we were shipped off to a local ground with a coach full of youths who looked like giants. I don't recall too much, except getting kicked a lot. It was a short career.

Next step was Barnet Sunday League side Victoria Park, another good side. The Friday and Saturday nights out and the after-match socials started getting more important than the games. So the career was on the slide.

I continued to play five-a-side, but more for fun really. But my love for the game never waned.

When my son, Luke, started playing, I had high hopes for him. Standing on the touchlines, shouting at the ref, we have all done it. Alas, another career that never got started. Fast-forward to the introduction of walking football. A new career is calling.

In 2014, I think most people saw the Barclays advert which featured walking football. I have to say well done to all concerned for bringing the game to people's attention, but I never really gave it a second thought.

With lots of free time, I got the usual questions from the wife: "What are you going to do with yourself?" My first thoughts were, I am not going shopping with you, that's for sure. Obviously I never said that to her, that would have been foolish, as you all know. So, after doing the DIY jobs around the house that had been waiting for years, playing golf, going to the Thursday Club with the boys – don't ask! – I started feeling a bit restless.

Somebody mentioned have you ever tried walking football? My ears were half-interested.

Barnet FC, my local club, who currently reside in the National League and have had some memorable moments in the past, were starting walking football sessions at the club. As it was only a fifteen-minute stroll, I thought I might give it a try.

I was a bit apprehensive at first and had to push myself to go. How exciting would a game of walking football be? I could not see it appealing to me. But I went. How wrong I was.

I turned up at The Hive, Barnet FC's ground, which has great facilities. Lots of grass pitches, lots of 3G pitches, cafes, bars. Walking up to the pitches, where I saw a lot of older gentlemen kicking a ball around, I honestly nearly turned around and headed home. But no, I pushed myself to the limit!

I was welcomed with open arms and met all the other guys. There were probably about fourteen people, and they could not have been nicer.

We had a great match, and I was pleasantly surprised at how well I fitted in.

On the walk home, I was thinking how much I enjoyed myself. Smiling, I thought, early days, but this could be really good.

As the week's progressed I looked forward to the Friday session for walking football more and more. The numbers grew, new friends were made. The social side was just as much fun as the football.

How the game has grown. At Barnet we have two sessions per week at present: Thursday evenings and Friday afternoons. We now have about sixty people in the club, with varying abilities, and everyone enjoys all aspects of the get-together.

The walking football club does fantastic work for charity, raising money for the Alzheimer's Society, Dementia Club UK, Age UK, and others. The club has a great social media presence on Facebook and Twitter. All of this overseen by Shaun Ashley Sherrick, who does fantastic work promoting all aspects of the walking football club.

As the team progressed, we started entering tournaments and had some success. We now have teams at over-fifty, over-sixty and over-sixty-five. Numbers are growing all the time, and long may it continue.

As the game grew, the WFA decided it was time to look at forming an international team in England.

You know things are going well and the game has a big future when this sort of thing happens.

Walking football teams were invited by the WFA to nominate players for trials to be held all over the country, with the aim of forming a national team.

Much to my surprise I was asked by the club manager if I was happy to be nominated for a trial. I replied, quick as a flash, "No problem."

Trials were being held all over the country for those nominated. Millwall, Solihull, Burnley and Cirencester were the venues. I was invited to the Cirencester trial. The trial was on Saturday 24 February 2018 at Cirencester Town Football Club. What a fabulous venue.

Lots of players from the south-east and south-west regions turned up for a series of drills and matches, with the goal for all being selection to the first England squad. Fabulous day, with lovely people, competitive games, all played in the correct spirit. The manager informed us at the end of play that he would be in touch with all players within the week.

I came away thinking I had done okay.

As the days went by, nothing. Refreshing my email inbox, nothing; the computer must be broken!

Oh, well. It was a great day, great fun telling everybody I had a trial for England, the laughter was deafening.

Then, a few days later, an email appeared from Stuart Langworthy, the England over-sixties team manager. It was like opening a letter from the tax man.

"CONGRATULATIONS. You have been selected for the England squad."

I nearly fell off the chair. Fantastic.

England over-sixties shadow squad versus Wales.

As time has gone by since the trial, I have become a regular member of the twenty-man squad. A great group of guys from all over the country.

Players in the first England over-sixties squad included Alan Kennedy, ex-Liverpool and England, and Tommy Charlton, brother of the famous Charlton brothers. As the game moves forward, I feel that more and more ex-professional players may start to enter the game.

Regional squads have now been formed in England. The idea being that those players who do well at regional level will have the opportunity to progress into the England squad. The pressure is on and nobody's place is guaranteed.

I am pretty sure that nobody can win 100-plus caps, like the giants of the game, Bobby Charlton and Bobby Moore.

The WFA England set-up is full of fantastic people who promote playing the game in the correct way. This is how we all want the game to be played. So all you walking footballers out there, have fun, respect the referee and your opponents and you will have many fun-filled years enjoying the game.

SIMON'S STORY

TWO YEARS AGO I RECEIVED AN EMAIL FROM Oxford United FC saying that they were starting a walking football club and inviting all over-fifties to go along.

I have never played regularly over the years, too busy watching Oxford United, home and away, and never really thinking I would be good enough. Anyhow, along I went with about thirty other guys, played in goal on a rock-hard Astroturf pitch, and loved it.

A few weeks later I played for the B-team against Portsmouth A- and B-teams on the morning of the Oxford versus Portsmouth league match. Both matches ended in draws.

When the Thames Valley league was formed, I made my league debut in 2017, autumn season, and at aged fifty-seven, I received my first-ever award as the club's B-team player of the year.

We now have three teams playing in the league and have just won our league with the C-team. Thanks to some good players in front of me, I did not concede a single goal in twenty games.

I feel lucky to represent the club I love and the game has given me a new lease of life. Now aged fifty-nine, I hope to have another ten years, as my 'career' has just begun.

It helps if the keeper can still
see the ball coming!!

CHAPTER FIVE

TEAMS FROM AROUND THE UK

Thank you for your details

Abbeymead Rovers Walking Football Club

Venue: Abbeydale Community Centre, Gloucester.
Session times: Monday, 10.30am and 8.30pm for
walking football. Sunday, 11am, for super
vets. Wednesday, 10.30am for disability
walking football.
Contact venue for more details.

Stuart Langworthy, the WFA over-sixties manager, explains, "The teams started five years ago with five over-fifties and an eight-year-old lad who was at Bristol City Academy. Like many teams at the beginning, we made up the rules as we went along.

"A year later we won the first-ever Gloucestershire league, got to the People's Cup Final, came third in the WFA Cup and second in the Champions Cup.

"Since then we have over-fifties, sixties, sixty-fives, seventies, disability and super vets, with over sixty members and still growing. The over-sixties have won the south-west Super Cup, with the fifties finishing third.

"We have three players who have had heart attacks, several who have had limb replacements (I have had a hip replacement myself), several with diabetes. We have one thirty-year-old with a heart condition, who is not allowed to play contact football. Our oldest player is seventy-six. We have a mouth almighty – Chris Fletcher, the face of radio, who is our real character. We have Terry Smith, whose father, Dave Smith, was a top-class referee and officiated at many games, including the FA Cup final and many European ties.

"We have a great bunch; the banter is fantastic.

"Louis wears a Sherlock Holmes hat to every session, nobody knows why! We are a housing estate in a rugby-mad city and punch well above our weight, but we love it."

Barnet Walking Football Club

Venue: The Hive, Camrose Avenue, Edgware, HA8 6AG.
Session times: Thursday, 7-8pm. Friday, 2-3pm.
Price per session: £3.
Contact venue for more details.

Barnet's walking football team was formed in 2015. Great facilities. Women players welcome.

Sixty members, great social side, enjoyed by all.

On a cold Friday afternoon, in October 2015, walking football started at The Hive, Edgware.

Mike Moate, enjoying a pint in the bar, was informed that walking football was starting the next Friday. So Mike, along with Peter Speroni – who, shall we say, are both the wrong side of sixty – went along with a couple of Academy lads, and Darren Petit, a friend of Mike's.

Mike says, "A game was played on a very small pitch with goals about a metre wide. Week by week the numbers increased as the word spread. Soon we had enough players to play on a bigger pitch and even a goalkeeper.

"We now run two sessions per week and play in many tournaments.

A fantastic walking football club, where everyone is welcomed with open arms. If you fancy having a go, just come along, you will have a great time, on and off the pitch."

I have been asked to mention a few things. Barry and Paul, two very good players, so they told me, played together in the 1970s, as did Lionel and Vince, who recently met up again out of the blue attending Barnet training sessions. The magic of walking football.

More recently, the Barnet walking football team represented the game by taking part in an FA film, *Heads Up*, which has Prince William and Gareth Southgate highlighting a new mental health campaign set to generate the biggest ever conversation around mental health.

Shaun Ashley Sherrick is the man who makes it all run smoothly, again, so he told me. Shaun does a fantastic job on the social media side of things for us, and I am sure we would not be where we are without his organisational skills.

Another good saying I have picked up along the way: 'loneliness is a silent killer'. You will never feel alone playing walking football, especially true at Barnet.

Barnet RIP (Running is Prohibited)

Venue: Bobby Moore Centre, Trott Road, Colney Hatch Lane, London N10 1ST.
Session times: Monday and Thursday, 11am–12pm.
Price per session: £3.
Contact 2ripwfc@gmail.com for more details.

Situated just off the North Circular Road, London. RIP Walking Football Club is supported by the Middlesex FA.

Howard Skolnick, a player at the club, commented, "Whilst the group consists predominantly of those who are aged over fifty, people with physical or mental difficulties of any age are welcome.

"We play friendlies and are members of the Central Middlesex FA friendly league which meet up every three months or so.

"The club only ask participants to respect their rules and other players. Everybody welcome."

Barnsley Pals Walking Football Club

Venue: Oakwell, Grove Street, Barnsley.
Session times: Contact Oakwell for details.
Price per session: £3.
Contact venue for more details.

Alan Crutch, who organises walking football for the Barnsley Pals, says, "All the players feel great about just playing the game they love, after hanging up their boots.

"Some great characters, including a seventy-eight-year-old who plays twice a week, who still tries to get away with diving headers. His response to being told it is a non-contact game, and no heading is allowed, is, 'I'm old-school, me.' The lads just sigh and count the bruises. He loves the sessions, but, unfortunately, no guarantee of safety if you are in his way.

"One of our best players is a female vicar.

"As well as our regular session, we play in friendlies, tournaments and turn up in unexpected places. The lads were asked to attend a ceremony commemorating the WWI Barnsley Pals Battalion. They turned up in their maroon shirts. Everyone was in full dress, complete with sashes, medals, etc. A few odd looks were given in the short procession."

Bedford Walking Football Club

Started in October 2012. The club runs five sessions, both evening and daytime around the Bedford area, including a women's only session.

Website: www.walkingfootballbedford.co.uk
Email: info@walkingfootballbedford.co.uk
Facebook: walking football Bedford
Twitter: @walkingfootie

After viewing Mike Bushell's BBC report on walking football in June 2012, friends Steve Williams and Ian Cole thought what a great idea it was.

They rounded up their football contacts and had a trial session. This was successful and regular sessions started in October 2012. As numbers grew it was decided not to limit ages, which meant sons and fathers could play together as well as friends from years past.

The Club soon forged strong links with both the Beds FA (to which they are now affiliated) and the Bedford Sports Development Team.

Steve and Ian say, "Interest continued and a second session was added at the start of the 2014 season. With walking football starting to be more widely known, people were coming from fairly long distances to join in.

"Regular day sessions were added in 2016, and the club decided to annually support a charity, Bedford Prostate Cancer Support Group. Voluntary donations were given each week by the players (over the last three seasons we have now raised over £2,500).

"It has always been about the recreational side of walking football for us, but we have always entered the FA/BBC People's Cup. After a couple of good runs in the 2015 and 2016 events, we again reached the finals in 2017 and after winning through rounds at Luton and Peterborough, the team took their place in the finals at Birmingham, where they lost on penalties in the semi-final.

"We added a fourth session for the start of our sixth season in September 2017, and we now have a total register of over 150 players.

"2018 kicked off with some unplayable weather, as 'the Beast from the East' took hold. Women's sessions were added, an area we have high hopes for.

"The players claim it's not an exact science and we do not claim that our sessions are perfect… it's about people kicking a ball about."

Belfast Walking Football

Venue: Templemore Centre, 96 Templemore Avenue, Belfast, BT5 4 FW. Telephone 07712 528282.

Session times: Wednesday, 5–6pm.

Contact alan.crooks@irishfa.com for further information.

The Irish FA Foundation say walking football is aimed at keeping men and women aged over fifty active and involved in football.

The foundation says, "There are many reasons why players can no longer play the traditional game and the opportunity to play walking football brings many benefits. Players enjoy the physical activity, the friendly competition and the important social aspect.

"The game has very specific rules that outlaws all running and allows no contact between players. Overhead height restrictions and indirect free kicks ensure that the sport is played safely with full consideration to the participants' age.

"Teams are either five- or six-a-side. As a result of these rules, games are played at a slower pace, often on state-of-the-art 3G artificial grass pitches, thus reducing the threat of pain, discomfort and injury, with players briskly walking through matches.

"This allows people who have loved the sport all their lives to once again safely get back to playing and also introduces the sport to people who perhaps have never considered playing before.

"The game is for males and females, and all the groups in Northern Ireland are open to new players.

"Why not give your local club a go as this form of the beautiful game continues to grow throughout the UK and beyond?"

Source: www.irishfa.com

Birmingham Walking Football Club

Venues: Beechcroft Tennis and multi-sports club, Beechcroft Avenue, Birmingham, B28 9ER; Solihull Walking Football Centre, Brick Kiln Lane, Solihull, B91 3LD.

Price per session: First session free. £5 thereafter.

Contact the above for session times.

beechcroftsportsclub@gmail.com.

solihullfootballcentre@gmail.com.

Birmingham Walking Football club have a fantastic set-up and are one the most respected clubs in the country. Paul Murtagh, England WFA over-fifties team manager, who is involved with the organisation of the club, says, "Walking football is a great way to start moving again, to have a kick-about, to make new friends and get fit whilst having some fun. An hour a week can really make a difference. It can help you lose weight, get fit, build strength, and develop better balance and core stability. Our sessions cater for forty- to seventy-year-olds, those less mobile due to illness or injury and ladies/women only.

"It really does not matter how old you are, what size you are, what background you are from or whether you are male or female; if you love football, this is the game for you."

Birmingham politely ask anyone interested in trying out walking football for the first time to contact them before attending sessions to avoid them becoming over-subscribed. Certain sessions are at capacity and unexpected increased numbers reduces enjoyment of the game. Please contact the venues to confirm availability.

AFC Blackpool Senior Seasiders

Venue: Playfootball, Garstang Road, Blackpool.
Session times: Over-fifties, Monday, 4.30pm–
    5.30pm. Thursday, 4.15pm–5.15pm (organised
    by Blackpool FC Community Trust Coaches).
    Monday (ages thirty-five to sixty), 6–7pm.
Cost: £4. Includes tea and biscuits.

Venue: Unity College, Bispham, Blackpool.
Session time (age thirty-five plus): Wednesdays,
    6–7 pm.
Cost: £4.

Stephen Hyde, secretary of the Seasiders club, told me the first session was launched in December 2013 at Blackpool Sports Centre with the support of the late Age UK Blackpool president, Jimmy Armfield, an ex-England and Blackpool player.

A competitive team emerged from those early days and played in various tournaments. They now have various age groups of teams (fifties, sixties, sixty-fives and seventies) due to an increase in numbers that attend the sessions.

In recent times the club has won the Football League Trust National Walking Football Cup, the Lancashire League, and have won the North West Regional Finals (WFU) for the third year in a row.

Bury Relics Walking Football Club
(The Relics)

Venues: Castle Leisure Centre.
Session times: Tuesday, 11am–12pm.
Price per session: £3.50.
Radcliffe Borough FC.
Session times: Friday, 10am–11am.
Price per session: £2.

Bury Relics (The Relics) were formed in early 2017. The team started playing friendlies in and around the area. After finding out about the Greater Manchester Walking Football League (GMWFL), they joined for the 2017 autumn season. At that point they had an over-sixties team, finishing second in the league, which was a great achievement.

The team now have over-sixties, over-sixty-fives and over-seventies playing.

In April 2019, women's sessions were started.

In May 2019, Bury hosted their first tournament on the pitch at Gigg Lane, Bury. Hosting eight teams from around the local area, it proved a big success.

The icing on the cake was in June 2019; the over-sixties team clinched the GMWFL (Greater Manchester Walking Football League) Division 2 title.

The team has brought great friendship to all who play. Most of the team are playing with some sort of injury most of the time. Some have long-term conditions, but all enjoy the banter and camaraderie the game provides.

People of all ages, abilities and handicaps are welcome at the Castle Leisure Centre sessions.

Source: buryrelics.com

Chesterfield Walking Football Club

Venue: The Akademy, Callywhite Lane, Dronfield, S18 2XR.

Session times: Monday, 11am–12pm. Tuesday, 7–8pm.

Price per session: £2.

This is where it all started.

John Croot, chief executive of Chesterfield FC Community Trust and non-executive member of the Walking Football Association, was the game's pioneer, who played a key part in introducing the game of walking football to the world.

John says, "In around 2008/9 as part of my role as CEO of the Chesterfield FC Community Trust I submitted a grant application to the Football Foundation Extra Time project to work with over fifty year olds. I was successful, and we received £20,000 in grant funding. Successful applicants were invited to a presentation meeting at Manchester United's former training ground, and now home of the MUFC Foundation, The Cliff in Salford, where we were informed of the criteria and outcomes required. We were told that we could engage over fifty-year-old's in activities based around social inclusion. Examples such as draughts, chess and light exercise were given.

On my journey back from Manchester I was giving some thought to the presentation and thought football always gets the numbers and as a football club Community Trust that is our core area, so how can I make the beautiful game accessible for the target age group? The first barrier was running, so how about if we walk instead of running and call it walking football? Then I thought about slide tackles and heading, which are clearly not suitable. The next day I spoke to my coaching and management team about the day and my thoughts. We set up sessions at Queen's Park Leisure centre in Chesterfield and had great numbers attending. A team was formed called Senior Spireites, and the sessions were soon featured on Sky Sports News. After this we were contacted by other club community trusts, councils, charities and leisure centre managers and so on, asking how they could start this new sport. A few years later the sport was featured in a TV advert and we were again contacted by organisations asking how to start sessions".

Ian Edmundson, a player at the club, says, "The club regard the fundamentals of walking football to be the three 'F's: Fun, Fitness and Friendship, and they try not to take it too seriously in their sessions, although everybody is trying to win during the matches. Most of the lads are still grateful to play at such an advanced age.

"We have one or two lads who find it difficult to forget how they used to play and still adhere to the Bill Shankly quote: 'That some people believe football is a matter of life and death. I am very disappointed with that attitude. I can assure you it is much, much more important than that."'

"We play at the Akademy, Callywhite Lane, Dronfield, S18 2XR, where there are four available 3G Astroturf pitches. This session is limited to new members over fifty years of age. Parking, changing facilities and showers are available, and we get together afterwards for a sociable chat and a drink. We are affiliated to the Walking Football Association and operate a 'turn up and play' session, costing £2. We have an evening session at the same venue on Tuesdays from 7pm to 8pm which, while aimed at the younger end of our membership who are still working during the day, is also open to all new members over fifty. If you are interested, just turn up and check us out.

"Hasland Walking Football Club, formed at the beginning of 2015, originally joined Senior Spireites as a satellite club in September 2015 for administrative reasons but although running as an independent session, it is now integrated into the club. They play every Thursday from 10am to 11am on the outdoor Multi-Use Games Area (tarmac surface) next to the pavilion in Eastwood Park, Hasland. The cost is £2 per session, including tea or coffee and biscuits afterwards in the pavilion.

"Again, if you are interested in joining the 'Hasland Has-bins' contact us, or just turn up and check us out."

Source: chesterfieldwalkingfootball.co.uk

Cove Walking Football Team (C.R.AP.)
(Cove Rapidly Ageing Pensioners)

Venue: Squirrel Lane, Cove, Hampshire, GU14
8PF.

Session times: Monday, 10–11am. Friday, 10–
11am, 8–9pm.

Contact venue for more details.

Cove Walking Football Club play in Farnborough and are famous for the Barclays TV adverts aired in 2014. This advert really brought the game to the public's attention. The club boasts 135 members and conducts three sessions weekly.

The club commented, "We were involved in the creation of an initial rulebook for the game, including a head height rule and definitions on what constitutes running.

"The club started out on a tarmac surface, before moving to a more suitable 3G surface, and have gone from strength to strength. Players from ages fifty to eighty-five attend sessions. All players have the opportunity to attend tournaments suitable to their level of play.

"We also like to play three-touch football, which is very popular. The three-touch game encourages a good pace to a match that sometimes does not happen when players have time on the ball."

Mick Quinn is a sports therapist and set up the over-fifties walking football club in Cove as a way of introducing late-stage rehabilitation patients back into physical activity.

All the principles and foundations of the club are built on peer-reviewed medical research with measurable facts and evidence, and not solely on individual opinions.

Mick also organises walking football tournaments in Italy, Portugal and Spain, for males over fifty and sixty-five. In September 2020, a women's over-forty competition will be added to the tournament to be held in Salou. Spain.

Congratulations to Mick and the Cove team.

Eastleigh Walking Football Club

Venue: Silverlake Stadium, Ten Acres, Stoneham Lane, Eastleigh, Hampshire, SO50 9NW.
Session times: Monday, 6.30–8pm.
Thursdays, 11.30am–1pm.
Price per person: £3. Free first taster session.

Eastleigh FC's walking football is an inclusive, sociable fun version of five-a-side football specifically for over-fifties, played on an all-weather 3G pitch.

The rules are adapted so there is no running, very little contact and kick-ins instead of throw-ins. A spokesman said, "With less stress on the body and no real sudden change of direction, the game allows participants to play without apprehension.

"The game is still competitive and play can be extremely tactical, favouring those players who take their time and read the pitch around them.

"We currently have two players who have represented England at over-sixty, James Trant and Ross Everton, along with Sandy Gilchrist who has recently been called up to the South-east regional squad."

In 2017, the over-sixties team won the WFA National Cup.

In 2019, Eastleigh entered the National Cup at over-sixty, over-sixty-five and over-seventy level. The over-sixty-five team losing on penalties in the semi-final.

The over-seventies team did the same. Winning their group and the quarter-final without conceding a goal, but losing to Portsmouth on penalties in the semi-final. So returning home empty-handed without losing a game, nor conceding a goal in open play.

Source: eastleighfc.com

Edinburgh City Walking Football Club

Venue: The World of Football Corn Exchange,
    10-11 Newmarket Road, off Chesser Avenue,
    Edinburgh, EH14 1RJ.
Sessions times: Thursday, 11am–12.30pm.
Price per session: £3.

Welcome to the home of Edinburgh City Walking Football, which aims to give older adults the opportunity to keep fit by taking part in a gentler form of the sport they love. It also offers folks the opportunity to meet a varied range of people in both a sporting and social environment and also to have a bit a laugh.

Information on the Edinburgh club's website, walkingfootballedinburgh.weebly.com, says, "Joining in a physical activity with a group of people your age can be a breath of fresh air, make you laugh and give you a good time. It's a great way to get out more, meet new people and feel better.

"Remember how activity used to feel?

"Remember playing football in the streets as a kid?

"Remember the feeling you once got from playing football at school/club with your mates?

"Who needs gyms? You don't."

There's no better way to achieve this than to play walking football with Edinburgh City.

Source: walkingfootballedinburgh.weebly.com

Feltham Old Offenders
Feltham Walking Football Club

Venue: Power league five-a-side, Nailhead Road, Feltham, TW13, 6SS.
Session times: Wednesday, 6–7pm. Sunday, 10–11am.
Price per session: £3.

Steven Lawrence, a player with the club, commented, "The club started in January 2016, and is open to all over-forties who love football, but can no longer play the traditional game.

"If you are younger than us – as most people are – please note that all friendly games against other teams or tournaments are reserved for over-fifty players.

"We play in the Central Middlesex League, which was started at our ground in March 2019. This is a friendly league played in fantastic spirit and enjoyed by all participating clubs.

"You would be hard-pushed to find a friendlier bunch of players who all enjoy the friendship and fun the game brings."

Fleetwood Town Flyers

Venue: Poolfoot Farm, Butts Road, Thornton Cleveleys, FY5 4HX.

Session times: Monday, 7–8pm. Wednesday, 12.30–2pm. Friday, senior's football, faster-paced session, 5–6pm. Sunday, 10–11am.

Price per session: £3.

George Greenall, a player at Fleetwood, says, "Football for the over-fifties in Fleetwood and the Wyre Borough has been going on for a number of years. The club aims to promote health and well-being to the over-fifties, and to encourage physical activity through walking football.

"The over-fifties were 2017 Lancashire League Series champions and also 2018 FA People's Cup national champions at St George's Park.

"The competitive form of the sport is played to the FA laws of the game, with matches lasting fifteen to thirty minutes. The standard of play is higher than in the training sessions and requires a certain degree of ability, tactical awareness and fitness.

"The excellent facilities at Poolfoot Farm offers a warm, friendly atmosphere and welcomes new players to come along and improve their health and fitness."

Grimsby Ancient Mariners

Venue: Bradley Development Centre.

Session times: Mondays and Thursdays, 10–11am.

Price per session: £2.50, savings can be made by direct debit or an annual fee (gives three months free).

Peter Cribb, general secretary of the club, says, "We were formed in 2012 by just three players and through their commitment and word of mouth, the numbers started to increase.

"By 2014, with over forty members, numbers increased steadily. The sessions are split into two distinct levels, known as the slower and faster games and we now regularly have over sixty players at each session.

"Currently the membership totals 125, and we are very pleased all players do not all want to play at the same time. In 2016, our greatest achievement was winning the People's FA Cup for Walking Football, a trophy that is on permanent display in the Grimsby Town trophy cabinet. Within the group, we have disabled players, cancer sufferers in remission, players recovering from heart attacks and strokes, widowers, and also some very good players. Recently, we arranged an over-seventies session that attracted twenty-five of our members, and a very enjoyable game was had by all.

"The secret to our success is two-fold: the minimum age is fifty-five, unless with some kind of disability, and two, a very active social side, including barbeques, quiz nights, golf days, day trips to the races, kayaking, Christmas markets and Christmas parties. We also hold social evenings where wives and partners can be involved." In 2019 they were awarded two sporting achievement awards, from Compass FM, an independent local radio station and the *Evening Telegraph*, the only club to win both awards in the same year. One of the players commented, "Walking football has given me a new lease of life after my wife died, and I received fantastic support from the members."

Grimsby Corinthians

Venue: Bradley Football Centre. Bradley Road,
    Grimsby, DN33 1QW.
Session times: Tuesdays, 10am–11am.
Price per session: £3. £10 club membership.

Grimsby Corinthians were formed in 2017. They have recently become an FA Charter Standard Club, becoming one of the very few walking football clubs to achieve this.

The team got together because of a desire for a group of players to be able to compete on a level playing field with other clubs in certain areas. The bulk of the initial founders were members of the 2016 FA People's

Cup Winning squad of neighbouring Grimsby Ancient Mariners.

So Corinthians were born and play once a week, with players required to be over fifty years of age. The club has grown far quicker than expected. They currently play in the Northern Premier over-sixties league and the East Riding FA League, along with other tournaments and friendlies. The club caters for all abilities and place players in matches to suit their needs.

The club's successes include becoming Lincolnshire over-sixties league champions, East Riding County Football Association (ERCFA) League champions twice (unbeaten over two seasons), and having several other tournament wins in Grimsby, Leeds and Hull.

In March 2019, the Corinthians were the hosts for the first ever LinxWF Community Charity Shield. A unique competition saw representative sides selected to play for South Lincs, North Lincs, Mid Lincs and the East Riding of Yorkshire at two age categories of over-fifties and over-sixties. A great day of walking football with South Lincolnshire being the victors.

The over-sixties team were also 2019 Northern Premier League champions.

Leyton Orient Walking Football Club

Venues: Score Centre, 100 Oliver Road, Leyton, E10.

Ive Farm Sports Centre, Walnut Road, E10. Outside, on 4G pitch.

Session times: Tuesday evenings (over-fifties)
– 6:30-7:30pm; Thursdays (over fifties)
– 11:00-noon and Fridays (over sixties) –
11am-noon. These sessions are open to all.
Women's sessions are on Thursdays – 1-2pm
(free) at Score Centre, and 6-7pm (£4).
Please note all sessions are at the Score Centre,
except Thursday 11am-noon, which is held
at Ive Farm.

Leyton Orient Walking FC is an FA Charter Standard
London FA Affiliated walking football club which was
started in 2015 by local walking football enthusiasts
and Leyton Orient Trust, with the primary aim of
getting those who are over fifty participating in a fun,
safe, social activity to address the known physical and
mental health issues of this age group. The club now
has more than 130 members registered, with regular
attendances of up to thirty people on each of the three
long-running weekly sessions. In addition the club
now runs two women's over-forties walking football
sessions. The Club has over-fifties, over-sixties, over-
sixty fives and women's teams competing in leagues,
tournaments and friendlies across the south-east of
England. The Club has close ties with Leyton Orient
FC with regular pieces in match programmes and with
walking footballers participating in match day events
on the Brisbane Road pitch.

The success of Leyton Orient Walking Football Club
has been very much founded on respect, enjoyment,

and mutual support no matter what the skill level of the participant.

This has also led to the club partnering with various community initiatives, engaging with local community groups and spreading the walking football message through coaching in schools and with overseas visitors.

If you want to get fitter, enjoy yourself and have some fun, please contact the club via e-mail at leytonorientwalkingfc@gmail.com.

Source: www.leytonorientwalkingfc.teamapp.com

Lisburn Ages Walking Football Club
Northern Ireland

Venue: Lisburn Leisure Centre.
Session times: Tuesday, 10.30–11.30am.
    Thursday, 7.30–8.30pm.
Price per session: £3.

Lisburn Ages Walking Football Club, from Lisburn, Northern Ireland, was formed in January 2017, by Bobby Jackson. Bobby says, "After speaking to the sports development manager at the leisure centre, we discussed our aims for the group. First and foremost, the aim was to get people out of the house, meeting people and have some exercise and fun.

"At our first session we had four people who played against some of the staff from the centre. Over the weeks, numbers progressed and at present we have thirty-four on our books. We have three teams: over-fifties, over-sixties, and over-seventies.

"When we are not playing amongst ourselves, we play friendly games, and lately we have been playing against a team of players who all originate from Sudan.

"I, along with my friend Ivor, have set up The Walking Football Federation of Northern Ireland. It is early days, but we are hoping to set up a Northern Ireland league shortly.

"We recently went to Salou for four days (warm weather training), taking twenty players, and had a great time.

"The social side is very important to all of us, as most of the players would probably be at home, some alone, so getting them out and about is fantastic.

"We have been approached by a mental health group, and they are going to include us in their events. Hopefully this could be the way we can help people, men and women, by introducing them to the game.

"Lisburn Ages are still in their infancy, but hopefully we will continue to grow and get more people involved, enjoying the companionship and friendship we get from our meet-ups.

"Every player cannot get enough of the game, and say they feel much fitter for it. One of the 'boys' who is eighty-two ran in the Belfast marathon and played with us the next morning. He contacted me later and said he would be away for a while as he was getting married and had just bought a motorbike to travel around Europe with his new bride.

"We currently have teams in Belfast, Ballymena, Coleraine, Lisburn, Newtownards and Newtownabbey."

Manchester Corinthians

Venue: Heywood Sports Village, West Starkey
    Street, Heywood, OL10 4TW.
Session times: Wednesday, 10–11am.
Price per session: £3.

Bill Murney started the Corinthians in 2017, after successfully managing Vintage Celtic, part of Stalybridge Celtic FC.

Bill commented, "The Manchester team has a core of thirty high-standard players from within a fifty-mile radius. We have two over-sixties teams and an over-sixty-fives team that won the National League in 2018. The team is progressing well and are regular tournament victors.

"We were hoping to gain another tournament victory in Spain recently, but the Sangria proved too good an opponent for the lads and the late nights took their toll.

"All the players love the sport, and the banter and camaraderie that go with it. We have players who have recovered from heart attacks and cancer, and walking football is proving the perfect tonic for all."

Sleaford Academicals Walking Football Club

Venue: Carres Grammar School, Northgate, Sleaford, NG34 7DD.

Session times: Saturdays, 9–10am. Tuesday, 6.30–7.30pm.

Price per session: £3.

Steve Morgon, of Sleaford, comments, "Founded in June 2018, the team started with just six members, which has now increased to thirty-eight, with ages ranging from forty-seven to seventy-four.

"The club recently received a £1,000 grant from North Kesteven District Council.

"Sleaford have clear-cut, undisputed proof that not only does walking football keep you fitter, it actually makes you grow younger.

"Tripps Mason, the club captain, recently underwent rigorous testing as part of his employer's staff health check programme and was found in conclusion, to have the body of… wait for it… a forty-eight-year old.

"If you compare this to the last time he was tested, he was advised not to walk home and was given the number of a funeral plan company to contact. This proves that Tripps is growing younger by the day. We all are, except one of us, Tam, as the game clearly has the opposite effect for people born north of the border. So, if this continues, the team are convinced that by the end of 2021, Tripps will only be thirty.

"So, if you are feeling your age at the moment, get yourself a pair of boots and join us before we all have to sign up for Sleaford under-twenty-one team, as we will be too young for walking football – Tam being the exception, of course."

South Ayrshire Walking Football

Football is alive and kicking in South Ayrshire.

No booking involved. Simply turn up at the following venues, with the appropriate trainers and clothing.

Each game lasts around an hour and will have the required water breaks. Don't hang around, get on the ball!

All the games have a referee.

If you are fifty-plus, get involved with the game at a venue near you.

Please check at a venue near you for more information.

- Monday, Ayr. Whitletts Pro Soccer 12.30–1.30pm. Cost: £4.
- Monday, Maybole. Carrick Academy, 6–7pm. Cost: £4.
- Tuesday, Troon. Muirhead Activity Centre, 8–9pm. Cost: £4.
- Wednesday, Ayr. Whitletts Pro Soccer, 6–7pm. Cost: £4.
- Thursday, Girvan. Hamilton Park, 4–5pm. Cost: £4.
- Friday, Prestwick. Caledonian Boys Club, 12–1pm. Cost: £4.
- Friday, Ayr. Whittlets Pro Soccer, 1.45–2.45pm. Cost: £4.

Plenty of walking football going on in Scotland. Look around, the game is everywhere.

Uxbridge Amblers Walking Football Club

Venue: Hillingdon Sports and Leisure Complex, Gatting Way, Uxbridge, Middlesex.
Session times: Friday, 7 pm-8 pm.
Price per session: £4

Founded in August, 2014, by Mick Geraghty and Mick Harvey, who do a fantastic job, the Amblers are a walking football club for the over-fifties with fifty members aged fifty to seventy-five years old.

The Club achieved FA Charter Standard status in 2015 and are conscious that walking football brings a new meaning to grassroots football with players getting exercise, socialising and reliving their youth through the beautiful game.

Mick Geraghty says "On the field the club develops recreational players in structured sessions to play competitions which has had great success, not only winning numerous tournaments in England but also in Italy".

The club has also been instrumental in developing session Activator and Referee courses with the FA and the Middlesex FA.

Off the field, the team work extremely hard to support both local and national charities, with over £18,000 raised to date.

The club also work with Dementia Friends of Hillingdon groups by delivering seated football and reminiscence sessions to over 100 people a week.

Wales

Yes, I know, Wales... hardly a club team, forgive me. Be honest, you thought I had forgotten you.

The game in Wales is growing fast, and the country has embraced the sport with sessions and teams everywhere – Merthyr, Cardiff, Swansea, Newport, Bridgend, Connah's Quay, Abercynon, Neath, Almwych, Carmarthen, Bridgend, Pontypridd, Tenby, Wrexham Rhyl, Prestatyn – the game is everywhere.

Having played against the Wales boys a few times, I can honestly say, what a great bunch of lads. Playing the game the way it should be played.

Wales – IWFF 2019 World Cup winners at over-60. Fantastic. A formidable force.

So if you are in Wales, look around, there will be sessions near you. Get fitter, have fun, make friends, you will enjoy it.

Watford Walking Football Club

Venue: Harefield Academy, Harefield, UB9 6ET.
Session times: Fridays, 7–8pm.
Please contact www.watfordwalkingfc for session
updates.

The club was established in 2015 with the aim of creating a community of walking footballers in and around the Watford area. The philosophy embraces both the playing and social benefits that walking football provides and therefore caters for people of mixed ability, from ex-footballers in, shall we say, their more formative years and those just wishing to stay fit and have fun with other like-minded people.

This activity is played on a non-contact basis in line with the interpretation of the Walking Football Association Rules, with whom we are aligned. At first, it takes a little getting used to, but once those natural instincts to charge around or run into open spaces are curbed, it can be really competitive, great fun and most importantly, immensely beneficial for your health and mental well-being.

For those of you that have played the beautiful game, still want to be out there competing at a pace that is much more suitable, this could be for you.

Source: watfordwalkingfc.co.uk

Weston Walking Football Club

Venue: Weston-Super-Mare Football Club. Winterstoke Road, Weston-Super-Mare, BS24 9AA.

Session times: Three sessions per week. Monday, 8–9pm. Tuesday, 10–11am. Friday, 10–11am.

Price per session: £3.

Please arrive ten to fifteen minutes before session.

3G pitch. Moulded plastic/rubber studs. No blades or metal studs, no flat sole trainers.

New players welcome.

No running. Minimal/no contact to minimise the risk of injury.

Apart from the weekly sessions, we run several teams for over-fifty, over-sixty, over-sixty-fives and over-seventy age groups, so that all players have the chance to play in leagues, friendlies or tournaments against players of similar age and ability.

Source: www.westonsmarefc.co.uk

Wigan Walkers Walking Football Club

Contact Wiganwalkersfc.co.uk for venue, session times and cost.

When Steve Halliwell hung up his boots after noticing it was taking a lot longer to get over his aches and pains from his regular five-a-side games, he was mooching around the house like a bear with a sore paw.

He then discovered walking football in Wigan. The sessions were being held on a day when he was not on duty for school runs for his grandchildren. After taking the banter from friends and family, who talked of Zimmer frames, etc., he turned up for a game on a Monday and was pleasantly surprised.

Instantly made welcome by a well-run club established in 2014, the members soon became friends. Steve says it is a pleasure to play every week.

"Many ill-advised folk said you will not get a decent sweat on. Well, they could not be more wrong.

"Even in the chill of winter, once the referee blows his whistle you are soon engrossed in the game. The game is classed as non-contact, and in the main, this applies, but like all sports, players push the rules to the limits, especially in the competitions we play in, both locally and nationally.

"The tournaments tend to be a tad competitive at times, but it usually always ends in a handshake at the end of the game. We have regularly held competitions for clubs in the north-west for over-fifties, over-sixties and over-seventies, and they are always over-subscribed.

"We have played in warm-up games at Everton against the England national teams, losing one and winning another, finishing third, behind the two England squads in a six-team mini-tournament.

"So, if you are over fifty, no matter what skill level, why not come down and see for yourself? I did, and have no regrets; I just wished I had done it sooner."

For more information please make contact at secretary@wiganwalkersfc.co.uk.

Wiltshire Walking Football

Venue: various venues throughout the county.
Session times: contact www.wiltshirefa.com.
Cost: contact your local club.

This article, sent to me by Wiltshire Walking Football team, is amazing. It shows what can be done with dedication and hard work.

Walking football started in Wiltshire on a cold October afternoon in 2014 with just ten players.

The session was set up by Tim Hall at Wilts FA and the Stanley Park Football Development team.

Two of the original players are still playing, including Tony Norton, who has been the driving force behind their growth as a volunteer, working alongside the Wilts FA and Wilts Council amongst others at several locations around the county.

They now have nine sessions a week across North Wiltshire, 330 registered players and an average 600 attendees a month playing walking football.

The sessions are all about a recreational turn up and play for fun and fitness, aimed at both males and females over fifty.

All the Rules and Good Practice guide is all the work of Tony Norton, based on the FA Laws of the Game.

Tony has become the go-to man for Wilts FA and Wilts Council in the Wiltshire area.

There are indoor and outdoor sessions, days, evenings and weekends, so hopefully something to suit everyone.

In June 2019, they trialled a friendly monthly inter-venue league with eight teams made up of regulars at the sessions.

Six players have now attended the FA referee workshops; others are still qualified FA referees and many hold FA coaching badges.

The entire organisation, registration of players, weekly mail shot updates, is done by Tony Norton with the help of lead volunteers at each session, who all report back to Tony each day with lists of attendees, etc.

With the need and desire for more competitive games by a small amount of players they ventured into festivals, friendlies and tournaments, both local, national and even abroad, again, all organised by Tony.

The year 2017 was quite successful for the competitive players, finishing fourth in a very strong thirty-two European team tournament in Almelo, Holland. They were also the first English team to take a referee to the tournament, in Keith Davis.

Their over-fifties team were beaten on penalties in the south-west regional finals of the WFU Nationals Tournament, where the over-sixties team fared better by winning their regional final and progressing to the national finals in Solihull, finishing fourth on the day.

Following the success and the desire to do better, Tony Norton and Keith Davis founded the Wiltshire Walking Football Club at the end of 2017, which has fifty-four members.

Tony Norton is the chairman/club secretary, as well as the kit man, assistant manager and captain of the over-fifties team.

He secured the club three kit sponsors, set up a club shop and arranged a facility for the club to call home.

They train twice a month, with wives encouraged to attend and use the meeting room for a social get-together, where they have even been known to watch the walking football.

In 2018, the club took two teams to Almelo, Holland, and were the first English team to take a female player. The team travelled with eighteen players and fourteen partners.

Before that, they had been playing in the FA People's Cup National Final at St George's Park, the largest walking football competition in the country, which is run by the English FA and the BBC.

On returning from Almelo, they appointed Alphie Archer as their manager and have since become the winners of the PlayFootball South-West Cup and the National Vintage Games held in Bath in 2018.

Alphie was having treatment for prostate cancer during their 2018 People's Cup run and was confirmed cancer-free in 2019. Alphie has now been inaugurated as a patron for the charity Tackle Prostate cancer.

The year 2019 saw Wiltshire Walking FC get to the People's Cup Finals at St George's Park for the second year running and finished third. They entered their first league, the Gloucestershire FA League, and finished second behind Weston-Super-Mare (WSM), by one point after going the whole season with just one loss and conceding just two goals.

Again they went to the Almelo tournament, taking two teams and finishing third and tenth respectively.

Also in 2019, Wiltshire Walking Football twinned with Brisbane Walking Football, and Wiltshire Walking FC twinned with Gold Stars Heracles, Holland. The first twinning of both walking football recreational sessions and competitive clubs.

Tony has been very instrumental in the growth of walking football, not only locally but on a national scale.

He was one of the original members of the WFU committee helping Steve Rich with his rules and competition structures.

He has been involved with the English FA in their rules development group.

For all his hard work he has been recognised many times:

- Wiltshire Public Health Awards 2014.
- Nominated: Improved physical activity in children, young people and/or adult's award.
- Nominated: Action to reduce health inequalities in community areas award.
- Wiltshire Public Health Awards 2015.
- Shortlisted: Tackling health inequalities in the community.
- Winner: Wiltshire FA Volunteer of the year 2016.
- Player Commendation: FA Mars Just Play Awards 2016.
- Nominated: The FA Respect Awards 2017.

- Appointed UK Ambassador for the Almelo City Cup in Holland in 2017.
- Wilts FA Independent committee member 2018/19.
- The FA and McDonalds Grassroots awards, volunteer of the year, Highly Commended 2019.

Now that is what I call inspirational.

I think we can all agree, what a fantastic achievement by Tony Norton and all the people associated with Wiltshire Walking Football.

Wolds Wanderers Walking Football Club

Venue: Caistor Sports and Social Club, Brigg Road, Caistor.
Session times: Wednesday at 11am.

The team was set up in 2017 by Bob and Sue Tubman with the primary aim to enjoy the game. Hoping for a queue to get in, Sue and Bob must be applauded for their perseverance when only three people turned up for the first session.

Bob says, "The team has moved onwards and upwards since then and now have an ex-archdeacon of Coventry Cathedral, an SAS chaplain who refereed a couple of games, notwithstanding a prosthetic leg, an ex-roadie for '60s band, The Animals, a real-life bodyguard for politicians, ambassadors and celebrities.

"Players have had the usual health issues, including one player who had a heart transplant." Bob drops this into conversation when some participants complain about a sore back or knee. Bob's mission is to try to recruit more female players in the future.

Good luck to Bob and Sue.

Many thanks to the teams and individuals for supplying information. Good luck and best wishes to you all.

Please check with all walking football clubs and venues near you for information and confirmation of session times.

Always get as much information from as many people as possible, with regard to suitable kit and footwear before you start.

Walking football is all over the country. There is a team for you. If you enjoy football, or want to get a little bit fitter, give it a try. You will enjoy it.

Go and have a look. Give the game a try, what have you got to lose. You have an awful lot to gain. Good luck.

Paul's story

P AUL STEPHEN IS A FIFTY-YEAR-OLD WALKING
footballer from Essex. A big fan of walking football.

Paul says that walking football has literally been a lifesaver for him.

This got me intrigued as to why he would say something as profound as this.

Paul says, "All my life I have suffered from chronic depression and since I have been playing walking football it has eased considerably. My depression normally comes out in anger and I used to do silly things like fighting in the street at aged forty-five, which was stupid," says Paul. "Thankfully, though, due to what walking football has given me, I am much happier. I have also made some great friends, which is something that would never have happened if I had not taken up the game."

After hearing this, I started to think about Paul's problems. What can I do to help?

I know: try and get more people playing the game, and help the NHS in a small way.

CHAPTER SIX

WOMEN'S FOOTBALL AND WALKING FOOTBALL

WOMEN'S FOOTBALL IS IN THE BIG TIME NOW. Women's walking football is starting to grow fast.

A really interesting book by author Gail Newsham, *In a League of Their Own! The Dick, Kerr Ladies 1917–1965*, recently caught my eye. This is a great story.

In the history of women's football, The Dick, Kerr Ladies are the most successful team in the world. They were formed at the Dick, Kerr and Co Ltd, munitions factory in Preston, during the First World War. These were ordinary factory girls who took the country by storm.

On Christmas day 1917, 10,000 spectators came to Deepdale, the home of Preston North End FC, to witness the start of the most phenomenal success story in the history of women's sport. Dick, Kerr Ladies notched up the first of many famous victories whilst raising £600 for wounded soldiers.

On Boxing Day 1920, 53,000 spectators packed into Goodison Park, Everton, to see the ladies take on St Helen's Ladies, with another 14,000 people locked out and unable to gain admission to the ground. Another victory was recorded for the team and an incredible amount of £3,115 was raised for charity.

During the war, the government appointed women welfare supervisors and sent them into factories to oversee the physical well-being of the factory girls and encourage the development of sporting activities. Among those activities was football, which became the official sport of the munitions girls. Almost every factory across the UK involved in war work had a ladies football team.

Incredibly in 1921, the FA was not happy with the ladies' success and banned them from using league grounds and effectively changed the women's game forever. The ban lasted for fifty years and was probably the biggest sporting injustice of the last century.

However the Dick, Kerr ladies continued to play football around the world until 1965, leaving behind a glittering legacy.

Now that is a fantastic story. Thanks, Gail.

In 2019, the Dick, Kerr Ladies held their third annual national women's walking fooball tournament, Birmingham winning the over-fifties and Newcastle winning the over-forties. Congratulations to Gail Newsham, the founder and organiser, as she continues to celebrate the famous Dick, Kerr ladies football team.

Can the women's walking football movement achieve something big? Yes, of course.

Women's walking football is slowly gaining more prominence. Many new teams appearing, weekly, means good news for all.

The WFA have also got big plans for the women's game. Successful trials have been held for the over-forties and over-fifties, and two squads have now been formed.

Hopefully, the formation of an England set-up, similar to the men, will push the game to greater heights.

I remember when the main form of women's football started gaining prominence. I was interested to see what it was all about. Would it be any good? I had my doubts.

Initial reaction to it was, it was okay, but I could not really see it gaining popularity among the masses. How wrong could I be? I love watching women's football. The improvement is massive; technique and tactics are there for all to see. After the women's fantastic showing at the World Cup in France in 2019, the game has arrived big time.

On a smaller scale, I remember travelling to Bedworth Town for an England training day. After the training, a few of us decided to have a sit in the sunshine and watch the ladies' match that was taking place in the stadium. After five minutes we were all talking about the quality of the football that the women were producing.

They were brilliant. Fast, technical, competitive. A real eye-opener for me.

I have no doubt the explosion of the women's game worldwide will continue. There is no reason why women's walking football will not also grow rapidly. The big push for exercise for all will continue. Physical and mental well-being is at the forefront of the media nowadays. So, ladies, if you are interested in getting fit, meeting people and feeling good, try walking football. Contact your local club. It does not matter what standard you are. It is fun for everyone.

There are numerous sessions around the country. Contact your local council or leisure centre for enquiries regarding walking football for women in your area. Here are a small selection of venues where sessions are currently being held.

Arsenal women's walking football.
Arsenal community hub, Benwell Road, London, N7.
Over-forties. Astroturf.
Sundays. £3.50 per session.

AFC Telford United women-only walking football.
AFC Telford United.
Bucks Head, Watling Street, Wellington, TF1 2TU.
Four all-weather five-a-side pitches.
Thursdays, 10–11am.
Ideal for those with lower activity levels or with low-risk medical conditions.
£2 per session. First session free.

Birmingham women-only sessions.
Beechcroft Walking Football Club, Hall Green, Beechcroft Avenue, Birmingham, B28 9ER.
Fridays, 7.30pm.

Chelsea Foundation walking football.
Xcel sport club, Walton, Surrey.
Friday mornings.

Crewe Alex LFC women's walking football.
Shavington Leisure Centre, Rope Lane, Shavington, Crewe, CW2 5DJ.
Thursdays, 7.30–8.30pm.

Crystal Palace walking football.
Monks Hills Sports Centre.
Thursdays, 7–8pm. Sessions are free.

Dover Athletic Football Club.
Lewisham Road, Dover, CT17 0JB.
Women only, forty plus.
Sundays, 10–11.30am.

Forest Sports Zone walking football.
Forest Recreation Ground, Nottingham, NG7 6HB.
Tuesdays, 6–7pm.

Herefordshire Walking Football.
Leominster, Bridge Street.
Mondays, 7–8pm.

Hereford, The Hereford Academy School.
Tuesdays, 7–8pm.

Lincoln City Foundation women's walking
    football.
Sincil Bank, Lincoln, LN5 8LD.
Saturday, 11am–12pm.
First session free. £3 thereafter.

Oxford United walking football.
Oxford Academy, Sandy Lane West.
Sundays, 2pm.

Port Vale.
Port Vale Academy Sports Hall, Off Hamil Road,
    ST6 1AW.
Tuesdays, 7–8pm.

Preston North End women's walking football.
Tulketh Community Sports Centre, Tag Lane,
    Preston, PR2 3TX.
Thursdays, 6.30–7.30pm.
£2 per session.

Tottenham walking football sessions for women.
Tottenham Community sports centre, 701-703
    High Road, Tottenham, N17 8AD.
Tuesdays, 6–7pm.
Free sessions.

Tranmere women's walking football.
Prenton Park, Recreation centre, CH42 9PY.
£2 per session.

To show how far walking football has progressed with regard to the women's game, Guernsey recently hosted the England WFA ladies team in a match billed as the first-ever Woman's Walking Football International.

match report by thewfa.co.uk
Guernsey 0, England 2

This historic match was played in dreadful conditions, but with a superb spirit being shown by both sides.

Unfortunately, due to days of torrential rain, the original venue, The Track, home of Bellgrave Wanderers, was declared unplayable as a result of being waterlogged. The committee in Guernsey worked a minor miracle and managed to switch the game and all the associated arrangements to the 3G at King George V playing fields.

The match was streamed live and encouraging numbers have watched it so far. Commentary was added courtesy of Brandi Mitchell, our guest from USA Women's Soccer, San Diego. Following an enthusiastic rendition of the National Anthem, which had been practiced on the coach journey to the game, the match kicked off.

England started very quickly and within the first few minutes Kelly O'Donnell opened the scoring with a crisp shot across the keeper from close range. England were passing the ball around very well with good movement creating several more chances. However, they were thwarted on numerous occasions by Emma Queripel, in goal for Guernsey.

Tracey Dudwell, Dee Reade and O'Donnell all had excellent shots well saved. Dudwell was holding the ball up well and creating chances for others and Reade was pulling the strings in the midfield area with Captain Lorraine Robinson mopping up everything at the back. Lydia Bleasdale played a lone role up front for Guernsey and was very lively without really being given any chances by the good England defence, although she did combine well with Jacqui Wheatley on many occasions, they got little change from the England team.

England made constant changes to enable all players to get equal grass time. This did not affect the shape or flow of the England team as they continued to pass the ball well and make chances. Mandy Walsh and Anne Fuller both had shots well saved and the pattern of the game with England probing and Guernsey defending superbly, with Kay Pires at the heart of a mean defence. Judith Darcy stepped into the England back line and was equally as composed and mean, thwarting many Guernsey attacks.

In the second half, it was pretty much more of the same. Ali Wayley controlling things at the back with Helen Graham creating chances for O'Donnell. The impressive Queripel, in the Guernsey goal, was proving a frustrating brick wall until O'Donnell scored her second with a fierce shot to give England some breathing space. However, this spurred Guernsey into action and Lydia

Bleasdale found a way through on the England goal to give Amanda Thompson, whose distribution was excellent all game, her first real test. She made an excellent first save but the ball span over her and was heading in until she scrambled back to hook the ball away before it crossed the line. In the final 10 minutes, Dudwell went in goal for England and she had to make a fine double save from Bleasdale. O'Donnell thought she had completed her hat-trick but it was disallowed for running.

The final whistle brought the historic match to a close – well refereed by Paul Carr and Andy Bisson. Well contested in dreadful conditions by both teams. It was a match enjoyed by the enthusiastic crowd and an occasion which will be remembered for the rest of their lives by all involved.

The main aim of matches such as this is to raise the profile of the game – we hope that many people enjoyed watching it and that, as a result, many more women will take up the sport. Those of us who are involved know all about the health and well-being benefits it brings. The players from both England and Guernsey are all excellent role models and they know how important it is to send out the right messages in order to get more people involved at grass roots level.

Huge thanks to all the Guernsey people for organising and running a very successful weekend.

CHAPTER SEVEN

THE IWFF (INTERNATIONAL WALKING FOOTBALL FEDERATION)

W HO ARE THE IWFF? HOPEFULLY I CAN TELL you a bit more about the organisation. Their dreams, aspirations and how they are progressing with the game of walking football.

The aim of the International Walking Football Federation is to unite the world of walking football with a definitive organisation that harmonises the international interests in the sport.

Adoptive affilliate member nations will form the foundation of the organisation, each embracing the ethos and principles of the federation in the further development of the international game.

Terry Rice, from London, is the founder of the IWFF, and in June 2019 organised their first-ever World Cup, held in London.

Terry was the founder of the TRA League for walking football in the UK before he decided to look at the game worldwide.

The World Cup over-fifties tournament was made up of fourteen representative teams competing for this coveted title: Argentina, Australia, Belgium, China, Cyprus, England, France, India, Italy, Portugal, Singapore, Spain, Turkey and Wales. An over-sixties tournament was also held.

Trials are being held around the world for countries to make their teams more competitive at international level. The IWFF have held trials for the women's international team, which is fantastic for the game. So, really interesting times ahead for all. All the activity going on around the game can only bring it to the attention of more people. More people playing, more people getting fitter and enjoying life. That is exactly what I would like to see. The IWFF are very proactive in their approach to the game, and to come up with a World Cup is no mean achievement. The organisation have big plans for the future of the game and are becoming well-known worldwide. Congratulations to the IWFF.

IWFF World Cup, June 2019, London. Over-fifties.

Group A	Group B
Belgium 14 pts	France 14 pts
Wales 11 pts	England 13 pts
China 9 pts	Italy 11 pts
Spain 7 pts	Turkey 8 pts
Argentina 5 pts	Cyprus 7 pts
Australia 5 pts	India 5 pts
Portugal 3 pts	Singapore 0 pts

Belgium, Wales, France and England progressed to the semi-finals.

Semi-finals
England 1 – Belgium 0.
Wales 1 – France 1
France win 3-2 on penalties.

Final
England 2 – France 0.

England crowned walking football over-fifties IWFF World Cup winners 2019.

IWFF World Cup, June 2019, London. Over-sixties.

Wales 14 pts
France 10 pts
Australia 9 pts
Spain 9 pts
England 7 pts

Final
Wales 1 – France 0.

Wales crowned walking football over-sixties IWFF World Cup winners 2019.

The IWFF organisation currently consists of Terry Rice, founder; Harry Engel, director for Europe; Derrick Smith, director for the Middle East; Xinmin Yan, director for China; Dr Dee Dee Mahmood, director for Asia; Ruudi Abrahams, director for Africa; Alan Templeton, director for Australia; Gavin Smaldon, disability director for walking football and Shaun Ashley Sherrick, head of media.

The IWFF's next venture, along with Walking Football Brisbane, is to hold an Inter-Continental Cup in Australia. Trials for the Australian team are taking place for over-fifties, over-sixties and over-seventies in the men's section, plus an over-forties for the women's section. The tournament is planned for June 2020. Attendees include Australia, New Zealand, Japan, Indonesia, Malaysia, Oman, Singapore, Thailand and Hong Kong, with more teams expected to be confirmed.

The IWFF are holding their first-ever European championship in Merthyr, Wales, in July 2020. The competition is for over-fifties, over-sixties and over-seventies. Plans are also being made for a World Cup in Barcelona in 2021.

Also coming soon will be the IWFF Copa Cup, featuring Argentina, Brazil, Chile, Costa Rica and Venezuela, along with big plans for the women's game and disability walking football.

The IWFF have recently reported that the first ever Women's World Cup will take place in Santa Ponsa, Mallorca, in May 2020. Check out their web-site for up-to-date information. www.theiwff.com.

Terry Rice has done a first-class job in his vision to spread the word worldwide about the beautful game.

Good luck to you all for the future

Source: www.theiwff.com

CHAPTER EIGHT

WALKING FOOTBALL WORLDWIDE

Did You Know?

Walking football is now played in forty-four countries and counting, including: Australia, Belgium, Brazil, Bulgaria, Cameroon, Canada, China, Cyprus, the Czech Republic, England, France, Germany, Ghana, Gibraltar, India, Ireland, Israel, Italy, Japan, Kenya, Malaysia, Mexico, Morocco, the Netherlands, New Zealand, Nigeria, Northern Ireland, Norway, Poland, Portugal, Qatar, Rwanda, Scotland, Singapore, South Korea, Spain, South Africa, Sweden, Thailand, Turkey, the USA, Uganda, Uruguay and Wales.

Source: www.thewfa.co.uk

The WFA and the IWFF are on a mission to get more countries participating in the game. The game is getting big. It seems that all around the world, once an individual hears about the game and decides to try it out, they are hooked, especially if they grew up playing football, and thought their playing days were over.

Here is a flavour of what is happening in some of the countries at the moment.

Australia

Football Federation Australia has recently announced it will launch a national walking football programme in association with the nine state/territory member federations. It is a two-year initiative based around a social, small-sided version of the world game. It is designed to get thousands of older Australians more active and playing the most popular club-based participation sport in the country. The announcement comes as part of an initiative aimed at the over-sixty-fives.

Source: www.ffa.com.au

China

Walking football is starting to emerge in Asia, and China is very hopeful of raising the profile of the game. A recent event at The Happy Valley Racecourse saw ex-Liverpool players Bruce Grobbelaar and Patrik Berger help with the promotion of the game. The event allowed members of the public try out the game for themselves.

A representative Chinese team participated in the IWFF over-fifties World Cup held in London in June 2019. A great performance saw them finish third in the group stage out of a group of seven.

The team secured two wins, three draws and one defeat in six games. A fantastic effort from a country that will be a force on the world stage in years to come.

Source: www.walkingfootball.com

Ireland

Walking football, or Danderball, as our Irish friends know it, is a big hit in Ireland and gaining popularity.

In June 2018, almost 100 players took part in a cross-border walking football event in Lisburn, Northern Ireland. The event was the second cross-border festival to take place following a similar event earlier in Dublin. Ireland have big hopes for the games as it grows and becomes more popular.

Source: ww.fai.ie

Italy

With walking football not as popular in Italy as in some countries, plans are in hand to grow the game over the coming years.

Last year, a representative over-fifties team played in the IWFF 2019 World Cup, finishing a creditable third place in their group of seven.

They have also played against the over-fifties and over-sixties WFA England teams. These games were the first-ever walking football internationals. Matches were played at Brighton and Hove Albion's Amex Stadium in May 2018, England winning both fifties and sixties matches.

Tournaments are held across the country, where teams from around Europe attend.

The Italian Masters Tournament is competed for every year. The last competition was held in the beautiful resort of Lake Garda in September 2019.

Portugal

Walking football is alive and kicking in Portugal. Albufeira, Vilamoura and East Algarve hold regular tournaments which consistently prove very popular.

East Algarve hold the International Albufeira Walking Football Cup every March.

There are also two international tournaments held in Vilamoura in May and October, hosted by Brown's Sports and Leisure Club.

Tournaments are held in Eastern Algarve on a fairly informal basis, with teams from around the Algarve and Europe competing in a relaxed environment with the emphasis on friendship.

Many teams from the UK have visited the Algarve for tournaments over the past few years, including Portsmouth, Preston North End, Derby County, Canterbury, Exeter, Sheffield United and Oxford, to name a few.

Portugal also sent a representative team to the IWFF World Cup held in London, in June 2019.

Scotland

Walking football was first introduced to Scotland in 2012, initially starting in Midlothian with early games also played in Tranent, through the Hibs Fit Fans in Training programme and has become one of the fastest-growing sports in the country. There are now over ninety-five groups with around 3,500 participants, covering most regions with an age range from early forties to ninety years of age.

Membership in the groups/clubs varies from ten to over 100, with new participants joining every week. Many of the groups welcome participants with disabilities, dementia, and those recovering from major illnesses, offering an opportunity to greatly increase fitness levels and improve social integration.

For more active participants, there is also the opportunity for competitive play, with many groups organising friendly tournaments and festivals. In June 2015, the first National Walking Football Tournament, organised by Age Scotland, took place in Edinburgh, attracting fourteen teams. In 2016, the entry was twenty-four teams and three years later, this event has now grown to include competitive tournaments at both over-fifty and -sixty-five age groups, plus a non-competitive festival that attracted a total of seventy-four teams, involving over 700 participants in 2019. The Scottish Walking Football Network started a steering group made up out of representatives of participating clubs and groups from across the country, and decided to create a governing body to develop and promote walking football.

Source: www.walkingfootballscotland.org

Wales

The game in Wales is proving extremely popular. The international teams are proving very formidable opponents in both over-fifties and over-sixties.

The Wales over-sixties team are the current IWFF world champions. A World Cup was held in London in June 2019. Wales defeated France 1-0 in the final. A fantastic achievement.

The over-fifties team also came close, losing on penalties in the semi-final to France.

Many teams have been formed in both north and south Wales, and the game is going from strength to strength.

Game On Wales is the award-winning sport programme delivered by the Coalfields Regeneration Trust.

There are still significant problems for the majority of Welsh coalfield communities such as fewer jobs, higher unemployment rates, more people with serious health issues, and a struggling community and voluntary sector.

For ten years through sport they have helped people in target communities gain new skills, achieve qualifications, find work and become more active, more often.

Game On Wales run regular 'turn up and play' walking football and 'football 5ives' sport sessions. In addition, they stage tournaments including the annual

Welsh Walking Football National (fifth edition in 2020) and deliver sport leadership courses. Something for everybody aged five to eighty-five.

I think the game of walking football can only improve with initiatives like these.

Source: www.gameon.wales

Chapter Nine

The Referee's Story

Here is a question. Why do more players not go into refereeing after retiring from playing? You would have thought players, particularly at the lower end of the game, who have not amassed millions of pounds, may be interested in this area. I am sure there are some, but not many. This has got me thinking now about sports around the world and how they get their referees. This sounds like a good book for me. Sorry, I digress.

Refereeing walking football is arguably the most important part of the game as it moves forward. More teams being formed means more referees needed. We must strive to have too many referees, rather than not enough. All trained to the same standards. As we all know, the game is going to be even bigger in the forthcoming years. You do not need a crystal ball to tell you that.

I just thought I would give a few opinions about refereeing generally, as the walking football phenomenon seems to be going from strength to strength.

Reading through different forums, the refereeing standards seem to be a common theme. I don't have any answers but feel a more positive attitude towards officials may be worth exploring.

Who would be a referee? Not me! Thankless task, most of the time. But where would we be without them?

When we turn up for a league game, cup game or tournament, we cannot play without a referee. You may have a young man or woman refereeing for the first time; give them a chance. Try and play the game how it should be played. Win or lose, enjoy yourself. Respect the referee. I was never the best throughout my life playing football, with regard to this aspect of the game, but I always try to think about this during games, not always successfully, but I am definitely getting there. I always try to mention this to my teammates along the way, sometimes getting quizzical looks returned to me. But I feel at our age we can get there. Whoever is refereeing, they will try to do their best. Why waste your energy berating them? The referee's decision is final. Show them the respect they deserve. Hopefully the refereeing standard will improve. Will this improvement help you respect the referee? The jury is out.

Managers and captains – how about telling your players this week to give the referee some slack?

Referees – get the players in a huddle before kick-off for one minute. Tell them what you expect from them during the game. Work together – everybody can learn from each other.

Now, what has amazed me since I was a boy is how do football players get away with giving referees such a hard time? How difficult would it be for world governing bodies to take a leaf out of the Rugby Union's book and educate players about behaviour towards officials? Is it better than it was? Maybe. Is it good enough? I would say no.

You still see top players showing dissent, showing the referee little respect throughout games. Is it fair to say that this trend will continue forever without change?

Rugby uses technology well. Match officials use the Television Match Official (TMO) to assist the referee on a regular basis.

In contrast, football has had to campaign for years to install goal-line technology. VAR (video assistant referee) is in use now, sometimes. But what about players' dissent towards referees?

Rugby players usually accept decisions without complaint. Captains and referee talk, but it is always with respect.

Walking football referees – imagine if you had VAR for a walking football match. That would be funny.

What do all you guys think about VAR? For me, and this was a quote I read, 'it is sucking the life out of the game'. Discuss. I know you will.

mick Hill — referee
(Grimsby Corinthians)

"Why do I do this, I often ask myself? Having refereed regular football following a long-playing career, I started playing walking football and came across a number of referees who I thought just didn't get walking football. Too much running, too much physicality, which caused tempers to flare. So I thought, I can do a better job than what I am watching. I reactivated my FA registration and started refereeing in competitions organised by the Lincolnshire FA. I got reasonable responses regarding my strict style and received invitations from wider afield and ventured further into the walking football community.

My contact with the FA enabled me to contribute to discussions on walking football law amendments and the current FA walking football referee workshops. As a result of this, myself and a colleague, Alan Rose, have formed the Walking Football Referees Association and initial support has been great. We are looking to develop the quality of walking football referees through discussion, debate, and possibly in the future through seminars and training events.

I have now been lucky enough to referee two FA People's Cup finals, 2018 men's and 2019 women's, plus a wide variety of leagues and tournaments including the Brown's Walking Football Tournament in Vilamoura, Portugal.

My hopes for the future? A unified set of laws, an improved definition of the walking law. Neither definition (in FA nor WFA law) is currently truly workable. Improved standards of refereeing, which in turn will improve the playing experience for all. A long and healthy experience, and back as a player more, as I turn sixty."

Antony Skelton

"The progress from a refereeing point of view has, in my opinion, been very good. The laws of the game are ever-evolving. I was an eleven-a-side, level 5 referee for many years, before switching to walking football. I attended a referee course run by the WFA. This course was a full day, and it ended up with each person who attended refereeing a ten-minute match. During this game, the referee was assessed by a qualified WFA referee and graded accordingly to either a club referee or a tournament referee.

From my point of view, until I attended the course, I had never played or, indeed, refereed in walking football, so I was correctly graded as a club referee. I have now progressed and been upgraded to a tournament referee within the WFA.

During my officiating, I have had the pleasure of refereeing Pele's Pearls, the over-fifties team who represented England, and indeed ended up World Cup winners, at the IWFF World Cup, held in June 2019 in London. A superb walking football team, playing the game exactly as it should be played. Walking, accepting the referee's decision without complaint, and playing with a great spirit. A fantastic team."

Les Burgess

"I am extremely honoured to have recently been appointed as Head of the WFA Referees Academy.

My predecessor, Bill Goreham, is going to be a very hard act to follow.

For those of you that don't know me, I am fifty-four, married with one daughter and two step daughters.

I am originally from Hereford but now live in Sheffield.

I also referee association football.

Although I live in Sheffield and spend a lot of the working week on the road (quite often away from home for several days at a time) I am chairman of a club in Hereford called Belmont Wanderers FC (which is mainly junior football but have a ladies' team and a veterans' team).

In June 2019, I was fortunate enough to have been selected as one of the officials at the Walking Football Association Euros at the Chesterfield Proact Stadium. This was an absolute honour as I was working with a fantastic bunch of referees (eight of us in all).

One of the first things that I would like to do in my new position is to hopefully train up more referee mentors and trainers, which will allow us to continue training up club referees, some of which will hopefully progress to tournament referees and eventually international referees.

I am extremely happy to discuss anything referee-related at any time, so please feel free to contact me with regards to courses or even if you just want some help with mentoring."

lesburgess@thewfa.co.uk.

Free kick, above head height

Chapter Ten

Summary

So, do we think walking football has a future? I hear a resounding yes all around, I am sure. The plan now must be for all of us to ensure we keep spreading the message about walking football, and the benefits that can be gained. Football, the best sport in the world, where you can start playing as a youngster and now continue playing as an oldster. Who would have thought?

If you fast forward, say, twenty years, could walking football become an Olympic sport? I am serious. The 2020 games, being held in Tokyo, are introducing five additional sports: baseball/softball, karate, skateboarding, surfing and sport climbing.

We must have a chance!

I started the book with some information about the NHS and social prescribing. I hope you found this at least mildly interesting. The idea of the book is to give a basic insight into the game, try to get more people playing, and making the point that there is something we can all do with regard to helping people, however small, with their health. Hopefully, this could lead in some small way to helping the NHS.

The NHS will always be there for you. Remember that phrase.

I thought I would sign off with just a few interesting facts and statistics from different regions of the UK with regard to ageing. We are all getting old. We need to keep healthy. See what you think.

Thank you all so much for reading the book, I really hope you found it a reasonable read.

One thing I would ask of you is to pass the book on to one of your friends (or ask them to buy it), who you possibly think may find it of interest. You never know, they might get the bug and have a go at the game.

For me, the best part of writing the book has been the comments and banter about it along the way, from so-called friends. Much of it unrepeatable! Fantastic. Please tell me what you think, when we meet up on the pitch. We can have a laugh; after all, that is what life is all about.

CHAPTER ELEVEN

THE AGEING POPULATION

Article by Handicare UK

The world's population is ageing at such a rate that the over-sixties now make up ten per cent, and by 2050 this is likely to rise to over twenty per cent. Keeping healthy is so important as we age, we can all help ourselves, which in turn can help the NHS.

In 2016, eighteen per cent of the UK population was over the age of sixty-five, according to the Office for National Statistics (ONS). The data has revealed that in some regions, as many as one in three people are over sixty-five and that the UK population is predicted to continue growing, reaching over seventy-four million by 2039.

Here are some statistics about the ageing population in the different regions of the UK. Read on to find out some other interesting facts about the over-sixty-five and over-eighty-five populations in the UK.

At first glance, London has a very low population of older residents, even though it is one of the most accessible places in the UK. In fact, eight out of nine areas with the lowest population of over-eighty-fives are London boroughs. Meanwhile, five out of ten UK areas with the highest proportion of over-sixty-fives are in the South West, one of the most remote parts of Britain.

Interestingly, a 2017 report by Public Health England highlighted the most deprived areas in the UK, and pockets considered to be 'more deprived'.

For example, areas in West Somerset, Mid-Devon, North Norfolk and Lincolnshire are all listed as 'more deprived'. The report states: "There is a widespread belief that people who live in the countryside are better off, both in monetary terms and in terms of health and well-being than those who live in towns and especially inner cities." Public Health England goes on to say that while this is certainly true for some areas, "for a number of years, there has been a growing realisation by national and local government, that broad-brush indicators, measuring the largely positive health, wealth and well-being of rural communities can mask small pockets of significant deprivation and poor health outcomes."

In this article, we will take a closer look at this data, what it tells us about the importance of accessibility and local services, particularly in rural communities, and what we can do to help older people and those with limited mobility.

South West

The rural South West, encompassing the counties of Gloucestershire, Wiltshire, Devon, Dorset, Somerset and Cornwall, is one of the most isolated regions of the UK. The Office for National Statistics (ONS) data shows that four out of the six regions with one in three people currently over the age of sixty-five are in the South West – East Devon, Christchurch, East Dorset and West Somerset. As of 2016, Christchurch also has the highest population of over-eighty-fives in the UK, at 5.6 per cent.

In such remote areas, local services are vital. Older residents need to be able to easily reach their GP, or hospital, and even amenities such as shops. Public transport links are an excellent way to ensure that older people with mobility problems who live in remote areas can access these amenities. Therefore, it's important that these services are maintained not just in the South West, but across the UK.

In Cornwall, one in four people are over the age of sixty-five. And this figure is expected to rise to almost one in three by 2036. Residents in areas such as the remote Lizard peninsula face a thirty-mile journey (one-hour drive) to the Royal Cornwall Hospital, and with the closure of community hospitals across the South West, the NHS is under increasing pressure. According to Public Health England, only fifty-five per cent of rural households compared to ninety-seven per cent of urban households are within eight kilometres of a hospital, and fifty-seven per cent of rural residents live within four kilometres of an NHS dentist, compared with ninety-eight per cent of the urban population.

Public Health England states: "Along with reductions in central government grants to local authorities, expenditure on adult social care services has declined and this has led to provision focusing on those assessed as having either critical or substantial needs. While the 'personal budgets' awarded to people in rural areas are lower, charges for social care are, on average, higher in rural areas, significantly so with respect to home care charges."

East Devon currently has one of the UK's highest populations of over-eighty-fives, at 5.2 per cent, and one in three people in the area are over sixty-five. In neighbouring North Devon, one in four people are currently over sixty-five, with this figure expected to increase to one in three by 2036. In West Somerset, the population of over-sixty-fives will have risen to forty-two per cent by 2036. With the added issue of a rapidly ageing population, it's important that local communities pull together to help older residents.

Peter Heaton-Jones, MP for North Devon, believes rural isolation is one of the biggest problems facing older people in the area: "The biggest challenge facing older people in my view is rural isolation and all the difficulties associated with that. From getting to the shops, to loneliness; we must work to ensure that local services and our communities do all we can to alleviate these challenges."

Despite these challenges, North Devon's MP believes the region's services are coping well with the ageing population: "It is widely known that North Devon's demographic changes are occurring earlier than for most of the country, and as such we have unique challenges. I think that broadly, local services are coping well. Northern Devon Healthcare Trust has been at the forefront of planning for these, and is working closely with Devon County Council. I have been impressed by the work that has been done to integrate service provision to alleviate pressures."

So what is being done to help older people? Peter Heaton-Jones says he has been urging central Government to increase spending on healthcare: "I have been lobbying central Government to increase local healthcare and local government spending. The government has provided real-terms increases to both of these sectors.

"I also campaign on care home issues. It is incredibly important that we have the right regulatory and complaints system in place so that families can feel confident that their loved ones are being treated with dignity and respect. I have worked with campaign groups to lobby Care Ministers on a range of issues, and I am pleased that the Department of Health has responded positively."

London and the South East

Despite a study by the Greater London Authority revealing that older Londoners are the fastest growing population group in London, the ONS study reveals that nine out of ten areas with the lowest proportion of over-sixty-fives in the whole of the UK are London boroughs – Hackney (7.3 per cent), Haringey (9.3 per cent), Islington (8.8 per cent), Lambeth (7.8 per cent), Lewisham (9.3 per cent), Newham (7.1 per cent), Southwark (eight per cent), Tower Hamlets (six per cent), Wandsworth (9.4 per cent). This trend continues in the over-eighty-fives age range with eight out of nine UK areas with the lowest proportion also being London boroughs – Hackney (1.7 per cent), Hammersmith and Fulham (1.9 per cent), Islington (1.7 per cent), Lambeth (1.6 per cent), Newham (1.7 per cent), Southwark (1.7 per cent), Tower Hamlets 1.5 per cent), Haringey (1.8 per cent).

Although London and the surrounding area have some of the lowest populations of older people in the UK, the city and the rest of the south-east, which consists of Berkshire, Buckinghamshire, East Sussex, Hampshire, the Isle of Wight, Kent, Oxfordshire, Surrey and West Sussex, are widely considered to be some of the most accessible places in the UK.

The London borough of Tower Hamlets had the lowest percentage of over-eighty-fives in the UK in 2016 (six per cent) and is predicted to have the lowest percentage in 2026 (6.9 per cent) and 2036 (8.8 per cent).

Although London generally has a younger population, however, parts of the South East do have a high population of older people. Almost a third of people in the district of Rother in Sussex, for example, are over sixty-five, and this is expected to rise to forty per cent by 2036. Rother also currently has the second-highest population of over-eighty-fives in the UK at 5.8 per cent and will have the joint second-highest by 2026 (5.8 per cent) and 2036 (8.8 per cent) with West Dorset. Oxford, on the other hand, has a notably low population of over-sixty-fives, at just 11.4 per cent as of 2016.

Wales

According to some research from the ONS on the Welsh Government website, the number of people living in Wales aged sixty-five and over will increase by 232,000 by 2041. This demonstrates that Wales, like the rest of the UK, will need to consider aiding older people in rural areas as well as those residing in its larger towns and cities.

In Wales, the places currently with one in four people over sixty-five are Powys, Conwy and the Isle of Anglesey and by 2036, it's estimated that the only four regions with less than one in four people over the age of sixty-five will be Newport, Cardiff, Swansea and Rhondda Cynon Taf.

By 2036, the Mid Wales county of Powys will have the joint third-highest population of over-eighty-fives in the UK at 8.7 per cent alongside West Somerset, while the over-sixty-five population in the area is set to be thirty-eight per cent, which includes the remote Brecon Beacons.

Cardiff, Wales's capital, has a relatively low population of over-sixty-fives compared to other parts of the country as it currently stands at fourteen per cent, although this is set to rise to eighteen per cent by 2036. In Swansea, nineteen per cent of the local population is over sixty-five, but this is set to rise to twenty-four per cent by 2036. The over-eighty-five population in Swansea and Cardiff is just three per cent, which demonstrates that Wales's two biggest urban areas have some of the lowest populations of over-sixty-fives and eighty-fives in the UK.

East Midlands

The East Midlands boasts a fascinating mix of large cities like Nottingham, Leicester and Derby with rural districts like Rutland, Rushcliffe and North Kesteven. As shown by the ONS study, this mix offers different challenges to authorities in the region.

By 2036, for example, one in three people in Lincolnshire will be over the age of sixty-five, yet only five per cent of the local population of North East Lincolnshire will be over eighty-five. In contrast, twenty-nine per cent of the population of East Lindsey is currently over sixty-five and this is expected to rise to one in three people by 2036.

The ONS research also highlights that, similarly to other large cities in the UK, Nottingham has a low level of over-sixty-fives and eighty-fives. Currently, 11.5 per cent of the population is over sixty-five and this is set to rise to just fifteen per cent by 2036. Only 2.3 per cent of the population is over the age of eighty-five and this could rise to 2.5 per cent by 2036.

Derby has a higher over-sixty-five population (sixteen per cent) than the other larger cities in the East Midlands, Nottingham and Leicester (twelve per cent), and by 2036 the population could increase to twenty-one per cent, which is very high when you compare it to Manchester (12.35 per cent) and Bristol (fifteen per cent).

West Midlands

Incorporating the key cities of Birmingham, Wolverhampton and Coventry, the West Midlands region (not to be confused with the West Midlands County) covers a large area, and its geography is immensely diverse. With its boundaries stretching into the rural counties of Shropshire, Herefordshire, and the south-eastern portion of the Peak District National Park, answering the question of 'How old is the West Midlands?' is not straightforward.

As of 2016, Birmingham's population of over-sixty-fives stands at just thirteen per cent and is only predicted to rise by a further three per cent by 2036. The suburbs, however, tell a different story. The districts of Bromsgrove, Solihull, Dudley and North Warwickshire are currently home to at least one in five over-sixty-fives. Shakespeare's home district of Stratford-on-Avon (encompassing Stratford-upon-Avon) has an even larger population of over-sixty-fives, at one in four. To the west, the population of over-sixty-fives in the Malvern Hills district currently stands at twenty-seven per cent and is predicted to rise to thirty-six per cent, over one in three, by 2036.

As well as the Malvern Hills, the West Midlands is made up of other rural areas, including the Wye Valley, Shropshire Hills, Cannock Chase and parts of the Cotswolds. As with other UK regions, the trend appears to show that most areas of the West Midlands will see their populations of over-sixty-fives increase to roughly one in four or even one in three by 2036, with the exception of more urban areas like Birmingham, Wolverhampton, Coventry, Leicester and Worcester.

East Anglia

Largely a rural area, the region of East Anglia – encompassing the counties of Norfolk, Suffolk and Cambridgeshire – is nevertheless also home to several large towns and cities, including Norwich, Cambridge, Peterborough and Ipswich. This contrasting geographic landscape goes some way towards explaining the significant discrepancies that exist in the region's demographic make-up.

More than one in three people in the East Anglian district of North Norfolk are over-sixty-fives, with West Somerset currently the only area of the UK home to a higher proportion of people in this age group. By 2026, it is predicted that, along with Rother in East Sussex, the district will also have the joint second-highest proportion of over-eighty-fives, at 5.8 per cent; by 2036, this figure is forecast to rise to 8.7 per cent.

The demographics are significantly different elsewhere in the county, with eight per cent fewer over-sixty-fives living in South Norfolk. Norfolk's coastal communities, meanwhile, are home to more over-sixty-fives than its inland areas, with every seaside town in the region (with the exception of Great Yarmouth) having at least one in four people in this age group.

Although the statistics are not as pronounced in the neighbouring county of Suffolk, officials there are nevertheless acutely aware of the challenges presented by the ageing population. In October 2017, council leader Colin Noble made reference to the prediction that, by the late 2030s, working-age people will be a minority in Suffolk. He noted at the time: "We have to look at the likely impact of all this. If we still think we can retire at sixty or sixty-five that could mean that we have thirty-five or forty years of retirement. What does that mean for us?"

Yorkshire and the Humber

Yorkshire, the UK's largest historic county, is renowned for its stunning countryside, charming towns and villages, and proud cultural identity. Its famous beauty, however, can sometimes mask the fact that there are significant pockets of both rural and urban deprivation in the county and surrounding region – something which is exacerbated by the rapidly ageing population.

Around one in four people are currently over the age of sixty-five in Yorkshire. In the areas of Craven, Scarborough, Hambleton, Ryedale and the East Riding of Yorkshire, the proportion of over-sixty-fives is predicted to rise to more than one in three by 2036.

Dr Lincoln Sergeant, North Yorkshire's Director of Public Health, discussed the issue of the county's ageing population in comprehensive detail in a report entitled 'Healthy transitions; Growing old in North Yorkshire'. Dr Sergeant's report emphasised that the county's wealthiest areas already have a life expectancy of thirteen years longer than those in the poorest, and he proposed that urgent action is required to address this disparity, as well as improving the treatment of over-sixty-fives in general: "A more radical rethinking of how we embrace frail older people as integral to our societies and communities is needed. The fact that someone needs care does not reduce their importance as a member of the community or diminish the contributions they still make."

North West

Despite its isolated areas, the South of England has long been considered more prosperous than the North, with London's position playing a large role in this. The North West in particular continues to struggle, and in 2016, research showed that ten of the UK's twelve towns and cities in greatest economic decline are in the North, despite the government's Northern Powerhouse initiative.

Life expectancy differs considerably in the North compared to the rest of the UK. According to the ONS, between 2010 and 2012, the average life expectancy for men in the North West stood at 77.7 years, compared to eighty in the South West. For women, the life expectancy for the same period stood at 81.7 in the North West and 83.9 in the South West.

The ONS data on the UK's ageing population reveals some interesting statistics. For example, as of 2016, the districts of Wyre and Fylde (above and below Blackpool) are the only two areas in the North West with one in four residents over the age of sixty-five. The city of Blackpool itself remains at twenty-one per cent. A recent report suggests that, from 2009 to 2013, men born in Bloomfield in Blackpool had a healthy life expectancy of just 47.1 years. Blackpool is considered one of the poorest cities in the UK.

With health apparently in decline in the North of England, what will this mean for the older population in these areas? By 2036, it is predicted that the only areas of the North West to have fewer than one in four residents over the age of sixty-five will be Manchester, Salford, Preston and Liverpool. Social care must be a priority in order to support the older population not only in cities, but also in the more deprived areas of the North West.

The rural area of South Lakeland in Cumbria is currently home to more than one in four people (twenty-eight per cent) over the age of sixty-five, with this figure expected to rise to thirty-seven per cent by 2036. The neighbouring district of Eden has similar statistics. Both areas encompass parts of the Lake District and Yorkshire Dales National Parks – two isolated areas with many towns and villages which can become vulnerable during winter weather. As with other remote parts of the UK, some older people in the heart of the Lake District can face an hour's journey to the nearest hospital.

North East

Combining Teesside, Wearside and Tyneside, the North East of England is perhaps most famous for its major cities – Newcastle, Durham and Sunderland. Despite its more cosmopolitan areas, however, some districts of the North East stretch into the remote North Pennines.

County Durham is currently home to one in five people (twenty per cent) over the age of sixty-five. By 2036, this is predicted to rise to one in four. This area is home to many small towns and villages in the North Pennines, which can be problematic for older people, as the nearest major hospital may be up to one hour and fifteen minutes away.

In 2016, the county of Northumberland was home to almost one in four people over the age of sixty-five (twenty-four per cent). By 2036, this is predicted to rise to one in three. Encompassing Northumberland National Park, the area has many remote towns and villages, many of which are more than an hour's drive from the nearest major hospital.

Scotland

Currently, the areas of Scotland with the highest populations of over-sixty-fives (roughly one in four people) are the Eilean Siar (twenty-five per cent), Argyll & Bute (twenty-five per cent), Dumfries & Galloway (twenty-five per cent), South Ayrshire (twenty-four per cent) and the Scottish Borders (twenty-four per cent). This contradicts the pattern in other parts of the UK, as the areas with the highest populations of over-sixty-fives are the areas that are home to Scotland's major cities. By 2036, it is estimated that one in three people will be over the age of sixty-five in most Scottish regions, with the exception of Aberdeenshire, Glasgow, Edinburgh, West Lothian and Midlothian.

In more remote areas, such as the picturesque Isle of Skye, older people must be prepared should they experience a fall or become unwell. The nearest hospital is in Raigmore, Inverness – 120 miles away. This slow journey takes roughly three hours by road. Fortunately, there is an air ambulance service available. Although Shetland, Britain's most northerly enclave, is a twelve-hour ferry journey north of the Scottish mainland, it is home to a major hospital. Currently, one in five people in Shetland is over the age of sixty-five, with this figure expected to rise to one in four by 2036. Further south, the Orkney Islands have a slightly higher population of over-sixty-fives, at one in four, predicted to increase to one in three by 2036.

Although the country has worked hard over the years to provide reliable health and transport services for older people in remote areas, Scotland is facing difficulties – there are now fears of a GP shortage in the country. According to a report by Third Force News, a Scottish news outlet for charities and voluntary organisations, a survey revealed that twenty-four per cent of surgeries in Scotland are advertising at least one vacancy. Age Scotland's chief executive Brian Sloan said: "The shortage of GPs is very concerning and could have a serious impact on older patients. We often hear from older people who have difficulty making appointments with their GP when they need them.

"This is having a knock-on effect on other parts of the NHS, increasing the chance of poor health outcomes and putting additional strain on our hospitals. Primary care physicians play a vital role in building relationships with their patients and identifying problems at an early stage, from symptoms of dementia to social isolation."

How you can help

It is clear from the ONS data that the UK's ageing population, particularly in rural areas, could be severely detrimental to the well-being of British people. Social isolation and loneliness, as well as deteriorating health due to poor transport links or an unreliable health service, are becoming increasingly likely as a result. However, with appropriate government funding, community support and thorough research, a positive trajectory can be achieved.

There are many organisations that offer volunteering and support services to older people including:

Age UK
0800 678 1602.
www.ageuk.org.uk

Royal Voluntary Service
0330 555 0310
www.royalvoluntaryservice.org.uk

Contact the Elderly
0800 716543
www.contact-the-elderly.org.uk

Handicare UK manufactures and supplies a wide range of mobility aids, thoughtfully designed to make everyday life easier for older people.
www.handicare.co.uk care

Always remember help is just around the corner for all of us. Stay fit, keep healthy, enjoy life and remember – there is always somebody there for you.

Addendum

THANK YOU TO EVERYBODY FOR YOUR SUPPORT and good wishes.

Special thanks to Martin Payne, caricaturist and fellow walking footballer for his help and advice.

Alan Crutch

Alan Crooks

Antony Skelton

Bill Murney

Bob and Sue Tubman

Bobby Jackson

Charlotte Moran

Christine Murtagh

Colin Mackay

Darren Hoyland

Dr. Gareth Lewis

Gail Newsham

George Greenall

Howard Skolnick

Ian Cole

Ian Edmundson

James Moran

John Croot

Judith Langworthy

Keiran Tilley

Keith Bibby

Keith Tyrrell

Kevin Ziants

Leon Dearns

Les Burgess

Mark Smith

Martin Payne

Mick Geraghty

Mick Harvey

Mick Hill

Paul Carr

Paul Murtagh

Paul Stephen

Peter Cribb

Pop Coogan

Richard Manning

Shaun Ashley Sherrick

Simon Jaggs

Steve Halliwell

Steve Williams

Sid Tobias

Stephen Hyde

Stuart Langworthy

Terry Rice

Tim Richens

Tony Norton

Trevor Ridley

bookguild.co.uk

chesterfieldwalking
football.co.uk

eastleighfc.com

fai.ie

ffa.com.au

gameon.wales.co.uk

handicare.co.uk

healthierfleetwood.co.uk

leytonorientwalking
fc.teamapp.com

irishfa.com

theiwff.com

thewfa.co.uk

walkingfootball.com

walkingfootballscotland.
org

walkingfootballedinburgh.
weebly.com

watfordwalkingfc.co.uk

westonsmarefc.co.uk

Abbeymead Rovers WFT

Barnet WFT

Barnet RIP WFT

Barnsley Pals WFT

Bedford WFT
Belfast WFT
Birmingham WFT
AFC Blackpool Senior
    Seasiders WFT
Bury Relics WFT
Chesterfield WFT
Cove WFT
Eastleigh WFT
Edinburgh City WFT
Feltham Old Offenders WFT
Fleetwood Flyers WFT
Grimsby Ancient Mariners
    WFT

Grimsby Corinthians WFT
Leyton Orient WFT
Lisburn Ages WFT
Manchester Corinthians
Sleaford Academicals WFT
South Ayrshire WFT
Uxbridge Amblers WFT
Watford WFT
Weston WFT
Wigan Walkers WFT
Wiltshire WFT
Wolds Wanderers WFT

Please accept my apologies if I have forgotten anybody.
Thank you one and all.